Also By Lorilee Lucas

The "Revive and Thrive" Series

Practical, evidence-based tools for personal transformation, authentic living, and creating a life that reflects who you truly are.

The Ultimate Self-Care Handbook

The Vagus Nerve Solution

Say No, Set Boundaries, Be Free: Companion Guide

Forthcoming

Speak Your Mind, Change Your Life

Polyvagal Healing Workbook for Trauma Recovery

The Ultimate Self-Care Workbook

The Ultimate Self-Care Challenge

SAY NO,
SET BOUNDARIES,
BE FREE

Create Guilt-Free Limits with Assertive Communication,
Find the Peace you Deserve &
Build Reciprocal Relationships
that Honor Your Worth, Values, Time & Energy

LORILEE LUCAS

Published by Everwell Publishing.
First Edition.

Paperback ISBN: 978-1-965625-07-1
Hardcover ISBN: 978-1-965625-08-8
E-book ISBN: 978-1-965625-06-4

Printed in the United States of America.

Disclaimer

This book is intended for informational and educational purposes only. It is not a substitute for professional medical, psychological, legal, or financial advice. Readers are encouraged to consult a qualified professional regarding their individual circumstances.

While every effort has been made to ensure the accuracy of the information presented, the author and publisher make no representations or warranties regarding completeness or suitability and disclaim liability for any outcomes resulting from the use or application of this material.

By reading this book, you acknowledge that the author and publisher are not providing professional services and are not responsible for any adverse effects or consequences arising from the use of the information contained herein.

For permissions, bulk orders, or speaking inquiries, please contact:
everwellpublishing@gmail.com

To those who crossed my path
and challenged the limits of my generosity.

By meeting you where you were,
I discovered the quiet strength of my own voice,
the shape of my boundaries,
and the depth of my capacity
for both compassion and truth.

Thank you for the clarity I could not have found otherwise.
I release the rest with understanding
and wish you peace wherever your path may lead.

CONTENTS

INTRODUCTION

RSVP to Your Own Life

I t's 3:00 PM on a Tuesday, and you are physically and mentally spent – not because you've been focused on your own priorities, but because you've been busy putting out everyone else's fires. You've spent the afternoon answering "quick questions" that turned into thirty-minute tutorials at work, juggling last-minute scheduling changes for your children's afterschool care, and policing a community volunteer thread that has devolved into passive-aggressive tension, just to keep the peace.

On the surface, you look like a hero. You are the reliable one; the one who gets things done. But underneath, you feel a low-grade hum of resentment. You realize that by saying "yes" to these small, draining interruptions, you've successfully avoided the important decisions and priorities waiting in your own life. The exchange is rarely equal. It is an exhausting paradox: you have become the most dependable person in everyone else's life, except your own.

Maybe your phone buzzes with an urgent request from a friend who always seems to be in the middle of a crisis. You sigh, your stomach tightening because you know exactly how this hour-long vent session ends: with them feeling lighter and you feeling like a dry sponge. Yet, the words *I can't talk right now* feel like a physical impossibility. You pick up anyway, effectively sacrificing your only window of peace because disappointing them feels more unbearable than neglecting yourself.

Or perhaps it's something heavier. You find yourself spending every weekend managing the logistics of an aging parent's care or picking up the slack of a colleague's chronic disorganization – not because you're the only one who can, but because if you stop moving, you might have to face the stagnant, overdue realities waiting in your own life.

This is the hidden psychology of the "Easy Yes." We agree because we don't want to be "difficult." We agree because we've been taught that our worth is measured by our usefulness. We agree because, frankly, fixing someone else's problem is a very effective way to procrastinate on our own.

The Weight of Being Everything to Everyone

If you feel the familiar weight of guilt the moment you think about setting a limit, you aren't just "being nice." You are likely operating in a state of self-abandonment. Whether you are an empath who feels everyone else's pain as your own, a "productive procrastinator" who uses chores for others to avoid your own dreams, or someone who simply doesn't know where you end and the rest of the world begins, you are here because you are exhausted. You are tired of the internal, "blink-of-an-eye" agreement that leaves you resentful by dinner time.

This book is the permission slip you've been waiting for. It's a guide to closing the leak of your time and energy so you can redirect it toward building the life you actually want to build.

Why I Know This Weight

If you feel like you're drowning in obligations, I want you to know two things: You are not alone, and you are not broken.

I didn't learn about boundaries in a classroom. I learned them in the ruins of a life I had spent decades building. In 2020, I faced a perfect storm that stripped me to my marrow. Lightning struck the redwoods behind my home, sparking a wildfire that consumed everything I owned. This came just months after COVID-19 decimated my career, taking with it the health insurance and financial security I needed to fight a mounting battle with systemic mold illness.

In the middle of this depletion, the most foundational pillar of my world, a twenty-three-year relationship, also ended. I had taken my vows seriously and fought hard to find a way forward together. For decades, integrity defined my identity. I believed in being a good person. I believed in loyalty. But crisis tests the architecture of a relationship without mercy and exposes what type of foundation a relationship is truly built on. As painful as it was to admit, I realized I had been sustaining something that could not stand without me.

In a moment of terrifying clarity, I decided to do something I had never dared to do: match the energy I was receiving. It was a simple act. I stopped doing the emotional heavy lifting, slowed down to ground my nervous system, and observed. With startling clarity, I watched the entire structure unravel. The relationship had depended on me bending, adjusting, and disappearing to hold the weight of someone else's world.

I had become a supporting character in my own life.

More Than a "No". A Way to Live

This book isn't just a collection of "scripts" for saying no, though you will find plenty of those here. This is a deep dive into the neuroscience and psychology of why we struggle to stand our ground – but explained in plain, human language. No jargon. No lectures. Just clear insight into how your brain processes fear and guilt, and how you can rewire those responses to favor your own well-being. Whether you identify as an empath, a recovering "people-pleaser," or someone who is simply exhausted from the toxic cycles of burnout, this is your roadmap.

Our Journey Together: Your Personal Invitation

I've organized this transformation into seven parts designed to take you from reactive (responding to everyone else's needs) to intentional (living by your own values). Think of the following chapters as the essential details of an invitation. We are going to cover:

* **What** boundaries truly are – and why they aren't "walls".

* **Why** they are one of the highest forms of self-care and self-respect.

* **Where** they apply: from your professional life to your most intimate connections.

* **When** to stand firm and when healthy flexibility serves you better.

* **How** to create boundaries using a clear, proven method.

* **Where they become real** – transforming how you live, relate, and lead.

- **What becomes possible** when you finally master this art.

The guest list for your life is about to change. You are cordially invited to the only party that matters: the one where you finally show up for yourself. RSVP yes. Let's have some fun.

I invite you to commit to this process, not because you "should," but because you deserve the peace that lies on the other side of a healthy limit. The potential for life-changing results isn't wishful thinking; it is a neurological reality. When you change how you communicate, you change your brain, your relationships, and your future.

Boundaries are not barriers. They are the bridges that lead you back to yourself.

Let's start walking.

PART 1

WHAT BOUNDARIES ARE

CHAPTER 1

UNDERSTANDING BOUNDARIES

Think about a friend who never seems to find the time to relax. Their calendar is an overflowing ledger of commitments, each one demanding a piece of their attention. They move from task to task with a practiced smile, but behind it lies a bone-deep exhaustion. When asked to take on one more responsibility, they say "yes" automatically, even as their mind screams in protest.

It's a familiar scene, isn't it? For many of us, we know that feeling because it is the air we breathe. We nod along while an inner voice whispers that our needs matter less than everyone else's. This is where the power of boundaries comes into play. It is a transformative concept that redefines how you engage with the world.

Boundaries are not walls meant to keep others out; rather, they are the invisible lines that safeguard your well-being and honor your personal space. They define where you end and another begins. These lines protect your integrity, ensuring that your mental health remains intact while facing the chaos of everyday demands. They serve as anchors in turbulent times, providing stability when the world feels uncertain.

Defining Boundaries in a Modern World

Boundaries, at their core, are simply the framework for how you engage with the world without losing yourself. They are limits you set to communicate what you are comfortable with and what you aren't. They allow you to engage with others without sacrificing your sense of self. They are your way of showing people how to treat you, rooted in honesty and authenticity, rather than control. They don't attempt to change others' behavior, they clarify what you will and will not participate in.

It's easy to confuse Boundaries with Barriers, but the distinction is extremely important. They move us in opposite directions.

1. **Boundaries** grow from self-worth and are built to define who you are. They are like a screen door: they let the fresh air of connection in while keeping the "bugs" out. They invite understanding and growth through clarity.

2. **Barriers** grow from fear and are built to defend who you are. They are like brick walls or shields, built from past hurts or fear. They might keep the pain away, but they keep love and connection away, too. Barriers invite stagnation and loneliness through isolation.

Choosing a quiet evening after a long week is a way to honor and recharge your energy. That is a boundary. Cutting off contact with everyone out of a fear of being hurt is a barrier. One invites understanding while the other closes the door to it.

Defining what feels comfortable creates space for reciprocal care and deeper bonds in relationships. They enhance mutual trust by setting clear expectations and allowing for open dialogue. In contrast, barriers act as defensive mechanisms that can stifle growth and lead to misunderstandings. Recognizing this distinction is important for developing healthy relationships and nurturing your personal well-being.

Beyond relationships, boundaries shape your relationship with yourself. They help prevent burnout, keep your focus clear, and remind you it's okay to put your well-being first. Choosing to set and keep them can bring a stronger sense of self and quiet confidence in your choices.

Mapping Your Boundaries

Take a moment to think about the "lines" in your life. Are they missing entirely, or have they become so rigid they are blocking the light? Use these questions to visualize how both boundaries and barriers are currently shaping your world.

The Leak: Where is a boundary missing?

Think of a situation where you felt resentful, drained, or "used," yet you stayed silent.

1. **The Moment:** Identify one specific instance where you said "yes" but your body was saying "no."

2. **The Saboteur:** What internal fear prevented you from drawing a line? (e.g., *Fear of being "difficult" or losing your "useful" status.*)

3. **The Cost:** How did this "leak" affect your energy and well-being the next day?

4. **The Architect's Move:** What would a healthy, respectful boundary look like in that scenario?

The Wall: Where have you built a barrier?

Think of an area where you have completely shut down or pushed others away out of a need for safety.

- **The Fortress:** Identify a relationship or situation you've entirely avoided or "blocked" to prevent getting hurt.

- **The Root:** Is this wall built on a current value, or is it a defensive reaction to a past wound?

- **The Distance:** Is this wall keeping you safe, or is it keeping you isolated and stagnant?

- **The Bridge:** What would it look like to turn this wall into a "screen door", keeping the harm out, but letting the connection back in?

Honoring your needs doesn't mean withdrawing from people. It gives you the freedom to engage with others in a genuine and confident way. Boundaries foster environments where respect is mutual, paving the way for deeper relationships built on honesty. As you keep exploring this topic, you'll find practical tools to speak your needs calmly and balance honesty with kindness. This skill deepens trust and strengthens the reciprocal ties you share with others.

When you set limits, you're doing more than drawing lines. You're shaping a life that reflects your values. Step into this work with openness, ready to see what's possible when you honor yourself and invite others to do the same.

The Scripts We Inherited

If you recognized a "leak" in your energy or a "wall" in your relationships during that exercise, take a breath. It is important to realize that these patterns didn't develop in a vacuum. You aren't "broken," and you haven't failed; you have simply been operating according to a set of outdated scripts.

Most of us were handed a "manual" for life that prioritized being helpful over being healthy. We were taught that our value was tied to how much we could carry for others, and that setting a limit was synonymous with being "difficult" or unkind. To move into the "center lane" of intentional living, we first have to unlearn the false rules that kept us stuck at the extremes.

Common Myths About Boundaries: Deconstructing the Manual

The belief that putting yourself last is a virtue is one of the most persistent lies we've been told. Many of us were taught that self-sacrifice signals strength, that endurance proves love, and that meeting everyone else's needs is simply what responsible people do. Over time, these messages become internalized, shaping our choices in ways we rarely stop to question.

These assumptions run deep and can quietly influence every interaction you have, from the requests you agree to without hesitation to the resentment you carry in silence. By naming these myths, we begin to loosen their grip. And once seen clearly, they no longer get to define the way you live.

Myth 1: Boundaries are selfish.

- **The Script:** "If I don't give 100% of myself to others, I'm being self-centered."

- **The Reality:** Setting limits isn't a rejection of others. It is actually an act of care and respect for those around you. By protecting your energy with boundaried self-care, you ensure that when you *do* show up, you are present, rested, and genuine rather than a hollowed-out version of yourself.

Myth 2: Putting yourself first is "wrong."

- **The Script:** "My value is measured by my usefulness to others."

- **The Reality:** When we prioritize everyone else's needs above our own, we eventually hit a wall of exhaustion and resentment. Eventually this leads to the "dry sponge" effect. Just as a reservoir cannot provide water if it hasn't been replenished by the rain, you cannot pour into others if your own energy hasn't been restored. Resting isn't a luxury you have to earn. You are allowed to protect your space and rest without apology or justification. Your well-being matters as much as anyone else's.

Myth 3: Boundaries will push people away.

- **The Script:** "If I say no, they won't like me anymore."

- **The Reality:** Clear limits actually reduce the "low-grade hum" of resentment. In a healthy relationship, boundaries increase safety because everyone knows where the lines are. It turns out that those who truly value you aren't looking for a "Yes-Man"; they are looking for a real person.

Myth 4: Boundaries mean cutting people off.

- **The Script:** "Setting a boundary is the same as ending a relationship."

- **The Reality:** Boundaries are the tools that allow relationships to *survive*. They help you stay connected on healthier terms. They are the "screen doors" that keep the connection alive and define how you relate without shutting people out. Barriers are what isolate us and cut people off; boundaries do the opposite by allowing us to stay connected in an authentic way.

Myth 5: Others should "just know" your limits.

- **The Script:** "If they loved me, they'd know I'm overwhelmed. I shouldn't have to say it. "

- **The Reality:** Expecting others to guess your needs is a setup for frustration – for you and for them. True accountability begins when we stop making others responsible for the lines we haven't drawn. Clear, kind words aren't an attack; they are a gift of clarity that help everyone feel safe and understood. When you withhold your limits, you are effectively asking those around you to navigate a minefield without a map. Most people would actually prefer to know where your boundaries are than to live in the guilt of accidentally walking all over them. Speaking your needs is an act of integrity that invites others to meet you in an honest, reciprocal space.

Myth 6: Boundaries are fixed and unchanging.

- **The Script:** "If I change my mind, I'm being inconsistent or weak."

- **The Reality:** Healthy boundaries are flexible. They shift as your life, roles, and energy levels change. True strength is knowing when to hold the line and when to allow for healthy flexibility based on the current context.

The Result of Living by the Myths

Holding onto these myths keeps us trapped in a cycle of guilt and fear. When we operate from the "old manual," every "No" feels like a betrayal. But when we see boundaries as guides that protect our peace, they become much easier to communicate.

Instead of acting from a place of fear (fear of being "difficult," fear of being "alone", "fear of upsetting others"), you begin to act from a place of clarity.

Take a moment to pause and ask yourself:

- Which of these myths feels like it was written specifically for me?

- How might my daily life feel lighter if I stopped trying to prove my worth through self-sacrifice?

By noticing these myths, you can start to shape practices that honor who you are and support the relationships that truly matter.

Boundaries in Real Life: Stories of the Shift

These myths aren't just abstract ideas; they show up in the quiet choices we make every day. Here is how two people found clarity by choosing honesty over obligation.

The Professional: Ella

Ella was the "Reliable One" at her design firm. For years, her value was tied to never saying no. When her manager asked her to lead four high-stakes projects at once, she felt the familiar panic of wanting to be "helpful" while knowing she was drowning.

Instead of swallowing her stress, Ella tried something new. She told her manager, *"I want these projects to be exceptional. To give them that level of quality, I can lead two at a time, but not four."* She expected a reprimand; instead, she got a partner. Her manager admitted he hadn't realized the weight she was carrying. By drawing that line, Ella didn't just save her own sanity, she improved the team's entire workflow. She stopped being a "hero" and started being a leader.

The Family Anchor: Ananya

Ananya grew up in a culture that believed loyalty meant being on call 24/7 for her family. She would cancel her own plans the moment a relative called with a "crisis," which often left her exhausted and quietly resentful. She feared that saying "no" would make her the "difficult" one in the family.

Slowly, she began to change the conversation. When a cousin asked for a last-minute favor that would have cost Ananya her only evening of rest, she said: *"I care about you and want to help, but I'm not available tonight. I can look at this with you on Tuesday."* The world didn't end. By holding that space, Ananya shifted the relationship from one of heavy obligation to one of genuine respect. She wasn't pushing them away; she was finally showing up with more interest and energy than ever as her true self.

Each of these stories shows something simple but often overlooked: boundaries aren't walls to hide behind. They're ways to live and relate more honestly. When you name your limits, you safeguard what truly matters and bring your full presence to the moments that matter most.

The Science of Boundaries

Our brains constantly sort through emotions, signals, and decisions. When it comes to boundaries, two key areas of the brain play a part:

- **The Amygdala (The Alarm):** Shaped like an almond and deep in the brain, this area triggers emotional reactions like fear and stress. It often fires when your limits are challenged, making it feel "dangerous" to say no or to speak up.

- **The Prefrontal Cortex (The Architect):** Located at the front of your brain, this area helps you weigh options and hold back impulsive reactions. When you pause to decide whether to say *yes* or *no*, this area helps you choose based on reflection rather than fear alone. By doing so, it supports clear and steady boundary-setting.

Neurotransmitters also play a role. *Cortisol*, the stress hormone, can make it harder to set limits by clouding judgment and draining your energy. On the other hand, *dopamine* and *serotonin* boost your sense of balance and reward, helping you view your own needs as a form of self-care rather than a source of conflict. This biochemical interplay highlights how our mental health and boundary-setting are intertwined, offering a foundation for sustaining emotional balance and well-being.

Beyond the biology of your brain, your personal history and psychological makeup also shape how you draw your lines. Several key frameworks help explain why protecting your space is so vital to your development:

- ***Attachment Theory***, for instance, suggests that early relationships shape how we perceive boundaries. Secure attachments in childhood often support the ability to form reciprocal and balanced relationships in adulthood. Conversely, those with anxious or avoidant attachment styles may struggle more with setting limits, seeking validation through compliance or withdrawal, underscoring the importance of nurturing secure attachments in fostering a healthy relationship with limits. *Real World Example:* Daniel grew up believing love meant always saying yes. Skipping a family dinner felt like betrayal. But the stress took its toll. Drawing on therapy, he told his mom,

"I love all of you, but I need tonight to rest." This step toward secure attachment let him trust that love doesn't vanish when he sets limits.

- **_Self-Determination Theory_** posits that autonomy, competence, and relatedness are critical for personal growth. Meeting these needs involves cultivating autonomy (the right to choose), competence (confidence in decision-making), and relatedness (respectful connections). Boundaries are the tools that protect these needs. *Real World Example:* In a busy office, Erika felt drained by constant interruptions. Wanting to feel capable and in control, she blocked off one hour each morning as *quiet time.* She told colleagues, "I'm offline for an hour, so I can finish priority work, then I'm all yours." This choice supported her autonomy (right to choose) and competence (doing quality work), while keeping relationships respectful.

- **_Maslow's Hierarchy of Needs_** places boundaries at the foundation of self-actualization. Without them, fulfilling higher psychological needs becomes challenging, as they provide the scaffolding for reaching our full potential. *Real World Example:* Leah treasures deep bonds but felt overwhelmed by late-night calls. Wanting to protect her time for rest and balance (foundational needs), she shared openly, "I love catching up with you, but I need to wind down earlier to sleep well." Together, they agreed on weekly catch-ups right after dinner time. Drawing personal lines helped her keep the friendship while honoring her own well-being.

- **_Cognitive Behavioral Theory (CBT)_** examines how thought patterns influence actions. A belief that setting limits is selfish can inhibit your ability to assert your needs. CBT encourages reframing these beliefs, recognizing boundaries as acts of self-respect that enhance well-being, empowering you to engage in positive behaviors that support emotional resilience and self-care. *Real World Example:* Omar once believed declining work made him selfish. Burnout proved otherwise. Through coaching, he challenged this belief, practicing: "I'd love to help, but my plate's full. Can we revisit this next month?" By reframing boundaries as a form of self-respect, not selfishness, he protected his health and the quality of his work.

The Impact: Evidence for Change

Honoring your needs aids emotional regulation by controlling stressors that trigger anxiety or overwhelm. By clearly defining what is acceptable, you reduce uncertainty and stress. This leads to increased emotional resilience and a greater capacity to handle life's challenges. In practice, this means fewer sleepless nights worrying about overcommitting or feeling resentful for saying "yes" to an unwelcome request, cultivating a sense of peace and satisfaction in everyday interactions.

Research supports these concepts robustly.

* *Longevity & Satisfaction*: Longitudinal studies reveal that individuals who consistently set healthy boundaries report higher levels of life satisfaction and lower levels of stress and burnout.

* *Clinical Success:* Trials involving boundary therapy show significant improvements in participants' mental health and relationship satisfaction. Furthermore, case studies illustrate that successful implementation can lead to transformative changes in personal and professional

realms, contributing to a richer and more balanced life.

Think of someone you know who handles limits calmly and kindly. They often seem steady and open rather than closed off. Their relationships flourish because they acknowledge both their own needs and those of others. They are living proof that boundaries are not fixed rules, but guides to help you stay rooted while you grow.

Stepping Into Your Power

In exploring the science of boundaries, it becomes clear that they are not just social constructs; they are deeply rooted in our biology and psychology. By understanding these mechanisms, we become better at maintaining them in a way that enriches our lives, offering us a framework to live with intention.

As you sit with this information, recognize areas where your own limits might be influenced by past experiences or current stress levels. Armed with this knowledge, you are better equipped to approach this not as an arduous task but as a natural extension of caring for yourself, fostering environments where understanding is paramount.

When we understand how our minds and nervous systems work, boundaries stop feeling abstract. That understanding gives us new language for living with intention and authenticity, turning boundaries into a practical way to support healthier, more honest relationships. From that foundation, a life shaped by honesty, trust, and love becomes possible.

PART 2

WHY BOUNDARIES MATTER

CHAPTER 2

THE IMPORTANCE OF BOUNDARIES

Now that you have a clearer picture of what boundaries are and how they shape your relationships, it becomes easier to see why they matter so deeply. Boundaries are not abstract ideas; they influence your energy, your sense of identity, and the quality of your connections with others. When they are clear and respected, life feels more balanced and relationships grow stronger. When they are weak or missing, stress, resentment, and confusion often take their place. Understanding the importance of boundaries reveals how these invisible lines quietly shape your well-being every da

The Psychological Need for Boundaries

Boundaries give you the space to share openly, without worrying you'll be judged or dismissed. When your feelings are acknowledged and respected, you're more willing to be honest, laying the groundwork for trust and deeper connection. In turn, respecting the boundaries of others invites the same care back, creating a reciprocal exchange that strengthens relationships.

They also protect your autonomy. They give you control over your life and decisions, empowering you to steer your course without external pressures dictating your path. Autonomy manifests in choices big and small, from selecting your career path to deciding how to spend a Sunday afternoon. By maintaining personal limits, you affirm your right to choose, reinforcing self-determination. This control bolsters your confidence, ensuring that decisions echo personal desires rather than others' expectations. They remind you that you have the power to shape your life according to your values and aspirations.

Your identity takes shape within the framework of boundaries. They define who you are by delineating what you stand for. They help articulate personal values, reinforcing identity through consistent actions and decisions. When you set limits based on what matters to you, they serve as a compass, guiding you through life's complexities. This process of identity formation helps you stay anchored through life's transitions. By understanding and practicing self-care, you cultivate a stronger sense of self, rooted in sincerity and integrity.

In social interactions, personal guidelines act as invisible lines that ease relationships and prevent misunderstandings. They establish healthy patterns of interaction by setting clear expectations for behavior and communication. When these parameters are defined, they simplify conflict resolution by clarifying acceptable conduct and fostering honest dialogue. In moments of tension, they act as a mediator, ensuring that disputes are addressed constructively rather than escalating into conflict. By structuring healthy choices, you promote an environment where relationships can thrive, grounded in mutual admiration and empathy.

Pages of Your Own

Take a few quiet moments to reflect on how boundaries are already shaping your life, even in ways you may not have fully recognized.

1. Think back to a recent situation where communicating your needs improved your emotional safety.

2. Notice a decision you made on your own and how it supported your right to choose for yourself. Did it feel like an act of self-trust?

3. Consider a value that guides your life and describe how your personal boundaries help protect it.

4. Think about an interaction where clear boundaries helped resolve or prevent conflict.

As you write, pay attention to what comes easily and what feels harder to name. There is no judgment here, only awareness. Each discovery is a quiet step toward understanding yourself more fully and honoring the life you are actively shaping.

The Hidden Costs of Weak Boundaries

Weak boundaries can quietly wear down your sense of self, one small compromise at a time. Over the years, the inability to establish strong boundaries can blur your sense of self-identity. It becomes difficult to define personal values distinctly, leading to codependency in relationships where your needs are perpetually sidelined. People-pleasing tendencies emerge, and personal goals are compromised as you prioritize others' desires over your own. This identity drift leaves you feeling like a stranger in your own life, unsure of where you end and others begin.

Emotionally and mentally, the cost is steep. Chronic stress and anxiety take hold as you repeatedly say yes when every fiber of your being screams no. Resentment builds beneath the surface, often leading to cycles of guilt and shame. Decision fatigue sets in as you're overwhelmed by the sheer number of small choices that should have been easy to make. This constant state of mental exhaustion wears down your resilience, leaving you vulnerable to emotional upheaval.

At work, the habit of taking on too much can blur the line between what's reasonable and what's too much. You may find yourself answering late-night emails, covering for colleagues, or saying yes to projects that leave little time for your own growth. Over time, this pattern can stall your career and leave you feeling underappreciated.

Physically, the impact is tangible. The stress from neglecting to establish healthy guidelines manifests in burnout and illness. Poor sleep quality and neglect of self-care routines become common as you prioritize others over yourself. Chronic headaches and digestive issues often arise from the constant tension you're holding onto. These physical symptoms serve as a bodily reminder that something needs to change, urging you to protect your personal space.

Your confidence takes a hit too. With lowered self-esteem, fear of rejection or abandonment lurks in every interaction. Assertiveness diminishes, leaving you feeling powerless in situations where you should stand firm. Relationships suffer as mutual understanding erodes, conflicts become frequent, and toxic behaviors turn into recurring patterns. In failing to prioritize yourself, you miss out on personal growth, creative freedom, and meaningful interactions. The delay in achieving life goals becomes the ultimate opportunity cost of weak boundaries.

Self-Care Through Boundary-Setting

Boundaries are acts of self-respect. They uphold personal dignity by protecting your internal well-being and clarifying what is yours to carry. When you establish healthy practices, you reduce the risk of overextension and create relationships that honor your limits. Caring for yourself in this way preserves your energy and integrity, allowing you to listen, help, and connect without resentment. Ask yourself gently, *What changes when I choose to care for myself before tending to everyone else?*

For many people, this question reveals an important truth: boundaries and self-care are deeply connected. You can't tend to your well-being without paying attention to your limits, and boundaries rarely hold when self-care is treated as optional or indulgent.

Self-care becomes practical when you check in regularly with your capacity across different areas of life, such as:

- Physical

- Mental

- Emotional

- Spiritual

- Social

- Professional

- Financial

- Intellectual

- Recreational

- Environmental

A simple daily or weekly check-in can help you notice where you may be stretching yourself too thin and where support or adjustment is needed. This kind of awareness creates balance; not by doing more, but by responding honestly to what's already there.

If you'd like to explore these self-care domains more deeply, *The Ultimate Self-Care Handbook* (also by the author) expands on this framework. The book includes a 16-page self-assessment that helps you quickly identify areas where extra support may be needed along with category-specific self-care ideas to prioritize those areas . It's meant to be a companion resource: useful, but entirely optional.

Learning to say no clearly and kindly is one of the most practical ways self-care and boundaries come together. You might begin with phrases like:

- "I appreciate the invitation, but I need to rest this weekend."

- "Thank you for thinking of me, but I have to focus on my current commitments."

Practicing these phrases, alone or with a trusted friend, can make them feel more natural. Over time, saying *no* stops feeling like rejection and starts feeling like care: for yourself and, ultimately, for your relationships too.

Saying No with Confidence

Choose a trusted person, or if you prefer solo work, imagine a familiar situation, and practice saying no in a few everyday scenarios such as:

- Turning down a work request that would overload your schedule

- Declining a social invitation when you need quiet or rest

- Setting a limit with a family member who expects your time or energy without checking your availability

As you practice, notice what happens inside you. Pay attention to the emotions that arise, along with any physical sensations like tightness, relief, hesitation, or calm. Notice whether your voice changes and whether your body relaxes or braces.

Afterward, reflect on what felt natural and what felt harder to say. You might ask yourself, *What made this easier? What made it challenging?*

By doing this, you build comfort with defining and expressing your personal limits as a form of self-care. Each time you speak openly about your needs, you strengthen your ability to live in alignment with who you truly are and nurture relationships grounded in trust, understanding, and genuine appreciation.

Boundaries and Personal Growth

Boundaries are like a mirror revealing your true self, encouraging self-discovery and genuine living. They act as a guide to understanding your deepest values. Without knowing what truly matters to you, life can feel like wandering without direction. By identifying personal values and priorities through thoughtful exploration, you build a compass for life's decisions, guiding actions to reflect your beliefs. This fosters authenticity, letting your true self shine in every interaction and choice made with intention.

When you set personal goals, boundaries act as quiet supports that keep you on track. They help you focus on what's important, instead of getting lost in distractions. Using the SMART approach (setting goals that are specific, measurable, achievable, relevant, and time-bound) works best when your limits protect the time and energy needed to follow through. In this way, your goals stay anchored in what matters most, turning plans into real progress.

Strong boundaries enhance decision-making skills by serving as a filter for choices. When decisions match your values, they become easier to make, reducing indecision and regret. By setting healthy limits, you give yourself the space to choose paths that honor your worth and support what you truly deserve. Later in this chapter, you'll see how boundary-based decisions play out in real-life situations, offering insight into how others navigate similar challenges. These stories will highlight how recognizing your own standards can shape decisions that honor your values and lead to rewarding outcomes.

Supporting continuous learning becomes seamless when limits are in place. They allocate time for skill development without overwhelming existing commitments. A balanced schedule emerges, blending personal and professional growth harmoniously. They create an environment where learning flourishes, free from the chaos of overcommitment. This space for growth encourages exploration, creativity, and adaptability, nurturing both personal and career advancement.

Emotionally, boundaries add strength. They help you handle stress by setting clear limits around what you can give and what you need to hold back. In disagreements, they guide respectful exchanges, helping you resolve issues before they grow. They keep interactions grounded in honesty and care, helping relationships stay healthy, whether at home or at work.

When your personal standards match what matters most to you, you don't just protect your energy. You give yourself room to grow, learn, and live in a way that feels true to who you are.

Emotional Resilience and Strong Boundaries

Building emotional resilience by protecting your personal space is like having a toolkit ready for life's unexpected challenges. When you establish boundaries, you create a buffer that protects your personal energy, helping you navigate stress without becoming overwhelmed. This layer of protection fosters a sense of control, allowing you to tackle emotional stressors with poise. Rather than succumbing to the chaos around you, they anchor you in moments of turmoil, providing stability and emotional regulation. They serve as a reminder of your capacity to adapt and remain grounded, even when external pressures mount.

Healthy boundaries strengthen emotional resilience by keeping you aligned with your values. When you're clear about your limits, you're less likely to be swayed by external pressures or expectations. This allows you to face emotional challenges with confidence and composure. Instead of reacting impulsively, you respond thoughtfully, supported by the structure your personal guidelines provide. Over time, this shift changes how your emotions move through you. Reacting less impulsively means fewer moments you wish you could take back and more choices you can stand behind. That consistency builds emotional resilience in a way that feels steady rather than dramatic.

Boundaries are indispensable in enhancing conflict resolution skills. They establish clear parameters for acceptable behavior, helping conversations remain considerate even in tense situations. With well-defined structures, conflicts can be de-escalated before they spiral out of control, preventing misunderstandings. They encourage constructive dialogue by fostering an environment where both parties feel heard and respected. This dissolves tension, allowing for resolution rather than escalation. The presence of clear lines reduces emotional defensiveness, paving the way for empathic conversations rather than adversarial exchanges. By setting these limits, you create a space where conflicts transform into opportunities for understanding and cooperation.

Boundaries also nurture healthy coping mechanisms, enabling you to recognize your emotional limits and protect your well-being. They prevent burnout by encouraging self-care practices that replenish your energy reserves. When faced with challenges, they offer the space needed to address issues without sacrificing mental health. This space becomes a sanctuary where healing and reflection occur, fostering resilience against future stressors.

Relationships thrive on trust and balance, both of which are strengthened by clearly defined personal guidelines. When emotional needs are acknowledged on both sides, understanding deepens and resentment is less likely to build. They provide a framework for interactions that honors individuality while fostering connection. Being clear about your needs and expectations enhances personal and professional interactions, helping relationships grow stronger and more fulfilling over time.

Boundaries in Trauma Recovery: Healing and Empowerment

Healing from trauma is a nuanced process that involves more than just time. It requires a safe environment where emotional wounds can gradually mend. Boundaries help create the safe spaces you need to feel secure and at ease. They act as a buffer, shielding you from further harm while allowing you to process emotions at your own pace. By setting clear limits, you cultivate an environment of trust with yourself, fostering a sense of security that is important for healing. This trust is not only about feeling safe with others but also about nurturing a reliable relationship with your own instincts and judgments by truly understanding what your intuition signals to you.

Rebuilding trust and safety begins with small steps, like engaging in gradual exposure exercises that gently challenge your fears without overwhelming you. These exercises, combined with supportive relationship-building, help restore your confidence in both yourself and those around you. As you slowly open up to others, personal lines ensure that interactions remain considerate, reinforcing safety and promoting healing. This gradual rebuilding process is akin to constructing a sturdy foundation, brick by brick, upon which a stronger self can stand resiliently.

Establishing personal guidelines is empowering for trauma survivors. It's about reclaiming autonomy and saying, "I decide what's right for me." By setting firm limits on triggering situations, you regain control over your environment. This empowerment is transformative, allowing you to navigate the world with renewed confidence. These frameworks act as a protective shield, enabling you to engage with life on your terms. They empower you to prioritize your well-being without apology, reinforcing your right to exist authentically and unapologetically.

Therapeutic practices often emphasize establishing healthy limits as a core component of trauma recovery. Grounding techniques help you stay present and centered, preventing past trauma from overwhelming the current moment. Structured boundary-setting sessions provide a framework for exploring personal limits and values, guiding you toward healthier interactions and self-awareness. These therapeutic insights offer practical tools for navigating the complexities of healing, ensuring that you feel supported and understood throughout the process.

In the journey of recovery, your personal standards serve as both the guardrails and pathways toward healing and empowerment, offering a customized roadmap tailored to your needs.

Everyday Stories: When Boundaries Become Real

Finding Your Own Compass

When Ana started her small business, she found herself constantly taking on extra work to please clients even at the cost of missing family dinners and creative time. One evening, she sat down with her journal and asked herself what truly mattered. The answer surprised her: family time and creative freedom were at the top, not endless hustle. Ana set a simple rule: no client messages after 6:00 p.m. It felt awkward at first, but over weeks, she noticed she had more energy, clearer focus, and renewed joy in her craft. That single boundary didn't just protect her time, but it also helped her line up her work with her deepest values.

Staying Steady Under Pressure

For Daniel, a teacher, constant requests from colleagues and students meant skipping lunch and leaving late every day. He realized exhaustion was making him short-tempered and less patient, which was something he never wanted for himself or his students. Daniel decided to block fifteen minutes midday, no exceptions, to step outside, breathe, and reset. At first, he worried this small act might look selfish. Instead, it helped him stay calm during chaotic afternoons and return to the classroom grounded. By protecting a slice of quiet time, Daniel discovered resilience doesn't always come from doing more, but from setting gentle limits that keep you steady.

Reclaiming Safety and Healing

After years in a relationship that left her doubting her worth, Maya struggled to say no to even small requests from friends and family. Therapy helped her practice phrases like, "I'd like to help, but I'm not able to right now." The first time she used it with a friend, Maya expected anger or disappointment, but instead got a simple, "I understand." Slowly, each boundary she voiced became a quiet act of healing. What felt at first like pushing people away turned out to deepen trust. For Maya, her personal lines weren't walls. They became stepping stones back to her own sense of safety and self-respect.

Together, these stories show what boundaries often look like in real life: small, imperfect choices that quietly change how safe, steady, and aligned we feel over time.

As we conclude this chapter on boundaries and their importance, remember they serve as both the guardrails and pathways toward healing and empowerment. Next, we'll look at how they shape your relationship with yourself, offering a guide to deeper self-awareness and care. Notice how honoring these internal limits could open the door to growth, healing, and a life that feels more aligned and complete.

PART 3

WHERE BOUNDARIES APPLY

CHAPTER 3

SETTING INTERNAL BOUNDARIES:

HONORING YOUR RELATIONSHIP WITH YOURSELF

Boundaries do not live in theory. They show up in the quiet choices you make throughout the day. Sometimes they guide an internal decision, like noticing when your energy is low and giving yourself permission to rest. Other times they appear in how you speak, how you respond to a request, or how much space you allow someone to occupy in your life. Some of these limits exist entirely within you. Others shape the way you relate to the people around you. Learning to recognize both is what allows boundaries to move from an idea into a lived practice.

Internal vs. External Boundaries

Think back to a moment when you felt stretched so thin that every outside demand felt like a threat to your peace. This is where the power of internal boundaries begins. More than just a set of rules, these are **self-regulatory** frameworks that govern your personal integrity. They act as the silent guardians of your emotional world, ensuring you remain true to your core beliefs, values and identity, even when external pressures mount. For empaths and people-pleasers, these boundaries serve as a compass, providing the vital distance needed to separate your personal needs from the emotions and expectations of others. By anchoring you in your inner world, they ensure that your "yes" or "no" is an authentic echo of your truest self, rather than a reaction to the noise around you.

Building these internal lines is a practice of mindful self-reflection. However, for many, "looking inward" can feel overwhelming if the internal world has historically been a place of chaos. You can begin with small, manageable check-ins. A simple practice is pausing to notice your physical reactions when a request is made. If you recognize a pattern of automatically saying "yes" even when your energy is low, you have found a vital data point. This awareness gives you the chance to respond with intention rather than habit. To do this, you may need to create a brief physical distance—stepping away from a screen or a crowded room—to offer your mind the quiet necessary to reconnect with what matters most.

External boundaries then act as the bridge between your inner clarity and the rest of the world. They shape how you interact with others by setting clear terms of engagement in your conversations, relationships, and work. While your internal boundaries keep you grounded, your external boundaries define how you share that grounded self with the world. By making space for fairness and mutual respect, they ensure that your everyday exchanges are balanced and sustainable.

To put it simply, your internal boundaries help you:

- Stay connected to your core values so you don't lose yourself in the shuffle.

- Identify when you are being "triggered" so you can choose a response rather than reacting in fear.

- Guard your energy reserves before they hit empty.

Your external boundaries help you:

- Communicate your limits with a voice that is both kind and firm.

- Protect your time at work and home, ensuring your "yes" is sustainable.

- Minimize misunderstandings by teaching people how to best interact with you.

Honoring your capacity often requires the courage to speak up. For a coworker, this might sound like: *"I need to finish this report first so I can give you my full attention. Let's talk at 2:00 PM."* This protects your focus while still valuing the relationship. In any professional setting, these clear limits are the primary defense against burnout.

Despite their differences, internal and external boundaries are intrinsically woven together. Internal boundaries and your internal world lays the foundation; it ensures your actions match your values and protect emotional reserves. This connection guarantees that when you set an external limit, it isn't just an automatic defense mechanism – a wall built out of fear -but a mirror of a genuine need. Understanding this delicate dance allows for a more authentic existence. When your internal world guides your outer interactions, you become more stable and true, even when the dynamics around you are constantly shifting.

Exercise: Building the Bridge

This exercise is designed to help you trace a line from your deepest values to your daily actions. Find a quiet space where you feel safe and follow these prompts.

Step 1: The Foundation (Core Values) List three personal values that feel non-negotiable to you (e.g., *Honesty, Peace, Reliability, Creativity*).

- **The Why:** Your boundaries are the "security guards" for these values. If you value *Peace*, but your phone is buzzing with work emails at 10:00 PM, your guard is off duty.

Step 2: The Internal Signal (The Test) Identify a recent moment when you felt a "ping" of resentment, guilt, or exhaustion. This is often the signal that an internal boundary was tested.

- **The Reflection:** What was the internal "rule" that was nudged? (e.g., *"I believe my rest is just as important as my productivity."*)

Step 3: The External Action (The Bridge) Describe how that internal feeling could be (or was) turned into a clear external boundary.

- **The Practice:** If the internal signal was exhaustion, the external bridge might be a script: *"I'd love to help with this project, but I can't take on anything new until Monday."*

Step 4: The Impact (The Sense of Self) Consider how upholding this boundary changes your "inner weather."

- **The Shift:** Does saying "no" externally make you feel more "solid" internally? Notice if there is a difference between the temporary discomfort of setting the limit and the long-term relief of honoring yourself.

By tracing this path, you move from reacting to the world to interacting with it on your own terms. Staying true to your values internally is the only way to build connections externally that are rooted in genuine trust rather than hidden resentment.

The Inner Critic: Transforming Negative Self-talk

In quiet moments, the inner critic often finds its voice. It can be relentless as it dissects every choice and amplifies every perceived flaw. While it often feels like a saboteur, it is frequently a misguided attempt at protection. It is an internal voice trying to keep you small so you remain safe from external judgment. Recognizing its presence is the first meaningful step toward reclaiming your internal limits.

Though the critic may claim to be "realistic" or "self-aware," there is a clear distinction: True self-awareness feels gentle, curious and understanding, whereas the inner critic feels harsh and accusing. Helpful processing looks for solutions; self-punishment only looks for blame. By learning to tell the difference between helpful processing and self-punishment, you give yourself the space to develop a kinder, more balanced inner dialogue.

Identifying the Patterns

To maintain your internal boundaries, you must learn to recognize the specific "scripts" your critic uses to keep you trapped. These self-authored narratives become powerful stories that confine you if they are left unchallenged:

- **Catastrophic Thinking:** This magnifies minor setbacks into seismic crises, making you feel as though one mistake has ruined everything.

- **Rumination:** This locks you into the past by endlessly replaying mistakes as if they were happening in the present.

- **Perfectionism:** This demands the unattainable. It sets you up for failure before the journey even begins.

- **Imposter Syndrome:** This convinces you that you don't belong despite glaring evidence of your competency.

- **Overgeneralization:** This takes one negative event and skews it into an all-encompassing truth about your worth.

Instead of trying to "fight" the critic, require strategies to foster a kinder self-dialogue. Reframe negative thoughts into productive, constructive beliefs. Instead of thinking "I always fail," shift to "I'm learning and growing through challenges." Identify and dismantle cognitive distortions. Those mental filters skew reality. Practicing self-compassion means treating yourself with the kindness you would afford a dearest friend in distress. When self-judgment lurks, pause and redirect your thoughts toward understanding and empathy. You might draft a mantra that echoes your core strengths or visualize past successes to counteract inadequacy. These realized achievements act as an anchor, keeping you grounded in facts rather than fearful stories.

Building this positive voice is an ongoing journey. Gratitude practices shift focus from what's missing to what's meaningful in your life. Affirmations replace hurtful inner scripts with words that honor your worth and remind you that you deserve care and respect. Mindfulness and meditation keep you present, easing the pull of anxious thoughts. Creative outlets like writing, painting, or music offer another path to express and reshape your inner dialogue, turning it into something softer and more supportive.

Through these practices, you cultivate a kinder internal world where growth feels possible and self-esteem can flourish.

Exercise: Mapping Your Inner Landscape

Color Your Inner Voice: This creative exercise helps you visualize the internal boundaries between your "critic" and your "compassionate self." By giving these voices a shape and a color, you move them out of your head and onto the page, where they are much easier to manage.

1. **Step 1: Create Your Canvas.** Draw a simple shape that represents you. This could be a human outline, a solid circle, or even just an abstract cloud. There is no artistic skill required; this is a map of your feelings, not a masterpiece.

2. **Step 2: Color the Critic.** Choose colors that represent the "weather" of your inner critic. You might use heavy grays for doubt, sharp reds for frustration, or a cold blue for sadness. Shade in the areas where these feelings usually "sit" in your body—perhaps a tight knot in the chest or a heavy weight on the shoulders.

3. **Step 3: Introduce Compassion.** Over the next few days, keep this drawing nearby. When you catch yourself practicing self-kindness or setting a healthy internal boundary, add a new color to the map. Choose shades that symbolize warmth and encouragement, like a soft gold, a vibrant green, or a calming violet.

4. **Step 4: Visualize the Shift.** As the week progresses, don't try to "erase" the critic's colors. Instead, let the compassionate colors wrap around them or soften their edges. This represents **integration**, showing that while the critic may exist, it is now held within a much larger, kinder

space.

Reflecting on the Map: At the end of the week, review your drawing. Notice how the introduction of new colors has shifted your perception. This practice helps you acknowledge criticism without judgment, gradually softening the grip of your inner critic. Each color and shape you add reinforces a kinder inner dialogue, one that acknowledges your growth and supports the person you are becoming.

Mindfulness and Boundaries: Staying Present and Aware

Mindfulness is more than a tool; it is a way of living that nurtures your inner guidelines. By choosing to stay rooted in the present, you keep yourself from drifting into the swirl of "what-ifs" and worst-case scenarios. This state of being allows you to observe your thoughts and feelings without judgment, creating a space between a stimulus and your response. That pause is where clarity lives, especially when your personal space feel tested. Mindfulness helps you become a kind observer of your own mind, making it easier to respond with intention rather than react on impulse. This practice is especially comforting for those healing from toxic relationships as it provides a secure mental sanctuary for healing and self-discovery.

Certain mindfulness practices make navigating personal limits feel more tangible. A body scan meditation, for example, guides you to focus on each part of your body, noticing sensations without attachment. This practice helps you identify areas of tension or "bracing" that signal where a boundary may have been compromised. By tuning into these signals, you learn to recognize your body's messages, safeguarding your well-being. Breath-focused exercises also help. By centering on your breath, you develop a sense of calm and control that helps you navigate stressful scenarios.

These techniques serve as havens, allowing you to check in with yourself and ensure your limits are acknowledged.

Emotional boundaries act as a vital filter between your inner world and the feelings of those around you. They allow you to remain empathetic without becoming a sponge for another person's distress. When these boundaries are clear, you understand that while you can support someone, you are not responsible for "fixing" their emotional state. This distinction is the primary defense against enmeshment, a state where your own peace becomes entirely dependent on the moods of others. You might recognize enmeshment as a sudden jolt of anxiety or a sense of "walking on eggshells" the moment a partner or friend enters the room. By maintaining an emotional limit, you stay anchored in your own calm, even when the people around you are in a storm.

Personal accountability is the commitment you make to uphold these limits, even when it is uncomfortable to do so. It is the practice of honoring your capacity and recognizing that your worth is not tied to how much you can endure for others. True accountability means checking in with yourself before committing to a new task and being honest about your energy levels. It involves moving away from the "culture of productivity" that suggests you must always be "doing" to be valuable. Instead, you accept the responsibility of protecting your peace, understanding that a well-maintained internal world is the only foundation for healthy, external connections.

As you integrate these practices, you move toward a life of profound intentionality. You begin to see that your internal boundaries do not limit your world; they define the space where you can exist with total honesty. By staying present, recognizing the voice of the critic, and holding yourself accountable to your values, you manifest a version of yourself that is stable and authentic. This alignment between your inner truth and your outer actions creates a sense of balance that remains steady even when the dynamics around you change. You are no longer merely surviving the expectations of others, but instead, you are finally living as yourself.

Emotional Boundaries: Protecting Your Inner World

Emotional boundaries act as a vital filter between your inner world and the emotional turbulence of those around you. Rather than a rigid shield that blocks everyone out, a healthy boundary is more like a permeable membrane. it allows you to remain empathetic and connected while ensuring you do not become a sponge for another person's distress. This is especially important for empaths who instinctively carry the moods of others as if they were their own. By practicing emotional differentiation, you recognize that you can care for someone without fixing what belongs to them. This is not a cold or distant act. Instead, it is the realization that your peace is a separate entity from the storms others may be weathering.

To preserve your well-being, you must learn to recognize the physical and emotional signals that your boundaries are being breached. Emotional enmeshment often disguises itself as extreme loyalty or deep love, yet it manifests as a loss of self. You might recognize it as a sudden jolt of anxiety in your chest when a partner walks in the room or a feeling of "fading away" as you prioritize someone else's crisis over your own basic needs. Red flags of emotional manipulation often include a lingering sense of guilt for asserting your needs or the exhausting habit of overshadowing your own feelings to keep the peace. Identifying these somatic cues, such as the tightening in your throat or the weight in your stomach, is the first step toward taking mindful action before your sense of self is eroded.

Establishing emotional guidelines takes practice and often begins with clear, neutral language. Phrases like "I need time to process my thoughts before discussing this" or "I respect your perspective, but I feel differently" help you express your needs with clarity rather than defensiveness. Instead of needing formal role-playing, you can build confidence through internal rehearsal. By mentally practicing these scripts in a quiet space, you prepare yourself to deliver them naturally when the moment arises. This process reinforces your ability to set limits with a calm authority, ensuring your interactions are guided by intention rather than a reactive fear of conflict.

Challenges in maintaining these boundaries often arise in close relationships where affection and loyalty can blur personal distinctions. It is paramount to overcome the guilt associated with communicating your needs by remembering a core truth: loyalty to another person should never require a betrayal of yourself. Many fear disappointing loved ones, yet prioritizing your emotional health ultimately creates a more sustainable environment for everyone. Being open about your need for personal space can foster a deeper sense of mutual respect. For instance, expressing how certain topics personally affect you can open pathways to empathy. These honest dialogues are transformative because they replace hidden resentment with unburdened, resilient bonds.

Consistency is the final key to this transformation. Regularly checking in with yourself helps you keep these limitations clear and responsive to your changing needs. Sometimes this requires the courage to have an uncomfortable conversation or to rethink how much emotional energy you give to a specific relationship. By staying present with your feelings and speaking them openly, you protect your inner life while still connecting deeply with others. In the long run, these efforts nurture relationships built on genuine care. These are the spaces where you can finally show up fully as yourself, confident that your identity remains secure even as you grow closer to others.

Personal Accountability: Prioritizing Your Well-being

In a world that moves at breakneck speed, self-care can slip to the bottom of your list. Yet it's what anchors your internal boundaries and keeps them strong. Your well-being needs steady attention. Without it, stress and fatigue can quickly overrun your sense of balance. Self-care encompasses nurturing your body and mind, yielding physical benefits like improved immunity, sleep and gut health, and a reduction in stress and anxiety. Self-care is a fundamental investment in your capacity to engage with life. By prioritizing yourself, you create a nourishing ripple effect. You enhance your ability to show up for others without depleting your own reserves, transforming self-care from a luxury into a necessary act of personal maintenance.

Many people feel guilty about putting their needs first, shaped by a culture that equates worth with productivity. Saying *no* or stepping back can feel selfish, as if your value depends on constant doing. However, your worth is inherent and is not tied to your utility. Understanding this truth changes how you see self-care from something optional to something integral. It's a choice that preserves your energy, keeps burnout at bay, and allows you to participate in life more fully. Over time, this shift can ripple outward, encouraging others to do the same.

Bringing self-care into your daily routine does not require grand gestures. It starts with small, practical strategies that protect your mental and emotional space. Scheduled downtimes, where you are intentionally unplugged from responsibilities, become sanctuaries of tranquility. Whether you choose to get lost in a book or take a quiet walk, these moments are essential for resetting your perspective. Creative activities like painting or journaling act as outlets for self-expression, allowing you to reconnect with what brings you joy. These practices replenish your spirit, ensuring you can meet life's demands with a sense of resilience rather than resentment.

To ensure your well-being remains a priority, consider designing a personal commitment that aligns with your specific needs. Start by identifying the activities that help you feel recharged. Choose goals that feel realistic within your current lifestyle, such as a brief morning pause or a weekly commitment to a hobby. Treat this plan as a living reminder to honor your own capacity, even when the world pulls you in different directions. Sharing these intentions with a trusted friend can provide a sense of encouragement, making it easier to follow through on the promises you make to yourself.

Prioritizing yourself is not an act of selfishness. It is an act of stewardship over your own life. You deserve to create a space where you can live, love, and connect from a place that feels steady and true to who you are. As we close this chapter on internal boundaries, remember that protecting your well-being is the foundation for a balanced life. Making self-care a part of your daily rhythm strengthens the ground upon which your personal space stands. With your inner world secure, you are now ready to explore how these limits extend outward, shaping your interactions and relationships in the chapters ahead.

CHAPTER 4

EXTERNAL BOUNDARIES:

NAVIGATING RELATIONSHIPS WITH OTHERS

Boundaries do not only exist inside you. They also take shape in the way you interact with the people around you. Every conversation, request, invitation, or expectation asks you to decide how much of your time, energy, and attention you are willing to give. Learning to navigate those moments with clarity is what turns boundaries from a private intention into a lived practice.

Professional Boundaries and Work-Life Balance

Workplaces often feel like a tower of deadlines, meetings, and sudden requests stacking up like Jenga blocks. Even in this chaos, remember that you are not alone in striving to achieve equilibrium. Mastering the art of establishing professional boundaries is imperative for safeguarding both your career goals and personal well-being. Defining your limits at work isn't about resisting responsibility. It's about making sure your career doesn't swallow the parts of life that keep you steady.

These standards might look like choosing not to check emails after hours or stepping away from work calls during dinner. When you keep your evenings for rest or hobbies, you reinforce the truth that your identity is far greater than your job title. This is not an indulgence. It's what helps you stay resilient and avoid burnout over time.

Balance often begins with small, consistent choices. Start by prioritizing your tasks and evaluating which items require immediate attention and which can wait until tomorrow. Try a digital detox now and then. Use *Do Not Disturb* during meals or walks. Stepping away from screens when the workday ends protects your focus and allows you to return to your tasks with a clearer mind.

Office politics can add another layer of challenge. Clear and honest communication is vital here. Share your availability so expectations stay realistic for everyone. When conflict arises, choosing to stay neutral helps you focus on solutions rather than being pulled into tension that drains your energy. It isn't always simple, but deciding where to place your emotional effort keeps you grounded. At its core, setting professional boundaries is about recognizing your own limits so you can show up fully in your work and in the parts of life that matter just as much.

Tracking Your Professional Boundaries

Use this simple audit to notice how you honor your limits at work over the next week. This exercise is designed to help you identify patterns and celebrate the moments where you successfully held your ground.

- **Step 1: Identify Your Non-Negotiables.** Make a list of

three to five limits you want to maintain. These might include taking a full lunch break, declining non-essential tasks after 5:00 PM, or keeping your personal phone put away during the workday.

- **Step 2: Record the Reality.** For each item on your list, note how often you respected the boundary and how often it was crossed. Be honest and curious rather than judgmental. This is simply data to help you understand where the pressure is coming from.

- **Step 3: Analyze the Patterns.** At the end of the week, look at your results. Which boundaries are holding strong, and which ones are consistently being tested? Notice if the "breach" comes from an external source or an internal impulse to over-deliver.

- **Step 4: Refine the Strategy.** Pick one or two small, realistic steps to strengthen a boundary that needs more attention. Instead of trying to fix everything at once, focus on one specific shift that would give you the most relief.

This practice helps you move from a reactive state to an intentional one. By visualizing your professional limits, you can gently plan improvements so your work life feels more balanced and truly supportive of your well-being.

Family Dynamics: Setting Boundaries with Loved Ones

Families come with love and history, but they also carry expectations that can weigh more than we realize. Parents may hold onto versions of you that no longer exist, and sibling dynamics can spark old patterns that quietly unsettle your peace. Identifying these long-standing roles is the first step toward protecting your sense of self while fostering relationships built on mutual respect.

Clarifying your limits with family requires a blend of honesty and warmth. You can use clear, simple language to communicate your needs without being harsh. Saying, "I need some time to recharge right now," acknowledges your need for space while still honoring the connection you share. When you speak from a place of calm, you move the conversation away from conflict and toward a shared understanding of how to best care for one another.

It can also help to weave boundary-awareness into your daily rhythm. Instead of waiting for a crisis, try incorporating simple, open questions into your regular conversations. These small touchpoints build a habit of transparency and keep trust strong. You might ask:

- "What is one thing we each need more of this week?"

- "Has anything felt particularly heavy or stressful lately?"

- "How can we support each other's personal space right now?"

Still, even the most compassionate honesty can meet resistance. Change is often uncomfortable, especially in families where habits run deep. Staying consistent is what allows these new patterns to settle in. If you find that your words are not being heard, remember that a boundary is not a request for the other person to change; it is a plan for how you will protect your own peace. This might mean stepping away from a heated discussion or limiting the time you spend in certain environments. Sometimes, if patterns remain stuck, seeking the perspective of a counselor can help the whole circle move forward. Ultimately, these personal guidelines are not meant to shut people out. They are designed to keep love healthy and sustainable, ensuring that family ties grow stronger because the individuals within them are respected.

Navigating Social Interactions: Boundaries for Introverts and Empaths

For introverts and empaths, social gatherings can feel like walking a tightrope. You often yearn for meaningful connection yet find large groups and constant noise physically draining. Choosing smaller, more intimate settings allows you to engage deeply without the overstimulation of a crowded room. In this context, solitude is not just a preference. It is a sanctuary where you can recenter and replenish your energy.

Drawing personal lines in your social life is about the power of the selective "yes." Gracefully declining an invitation requires honesty rather than an elaborate excuse. A straightforward, "I appreciate the invite, but I need some downtime," conveys your needs without causing offense. Additionally, setting a time limit on your attendance allows you to enjoy the interaction without overstaying your comfort zone. By doing this, you honor your own capacity while still showing up for the people you care about.

When you know a gathering might feel overwhelming, having a practical exit strategy is essential. This might mean driving your own vehicle so you can leave when your energy dips, or letting the host know ahead of time that you can only stay for an hour. Alongside these functional boundaries, you can use sensory tools to stay grounded. Noise-canceling headphones for the commute home or a calming scent on your wrist can help you transition back to a state of calm when the world feels too loud.

It also helps to build a circle of friends who cherish your personal space without requiring a constant explanation. Look for people who appreciate quiet moments as much as conversation and who do not equate your need for rest with a lack of interest. Within these relationships, being open about your comfort levels encourages others to do the same. Over time, these friendships become places where you can fully be yourself without the pressure to perform or hide your fatigue.

If you often feel torn between the desire to join in and the need for space, try a brief post-event reflection to help you notice your patterns. Ask yourself:

* What parts of the event felt nourishing?

* At what specific point did I feel my energy begin to drop?

* What small change would make me feel more secure next time?

This gentle check-in helps you move away from viewing social life as an obligation. Instead, it becomes a curated part of your life that supports, rather than drains, your well-being.

Healthy Relationship Boundaries

Sustainable boundaries in your relationships create the space where trust and genuine care can flourish. Rather than shutting people out, they establish a secure environment where everyone feels valued. Sometimes, this simply means recognizing when a partner or friend needs solitude or prefers to keep certain parts of their life private. Open dialogue is the foundation of this process, as it allows both sides to share their needs without the fear of being judged. This transparency ensures that trust grows naturally as the relationship deepens.

Clear expectations act as a safeguard against the quiet resentment that often builds when needs go unspoken. When you voice your limits, you protect the relationship from the strain of feeling overwhelmed or underappreciated. Over time, this clarity helps both individuals grow while staying deeply connected. Supporting each other's independence keeps the bond steady and ensures that your partnership is based on mutual respect rather than a loss of self.

To maintain these interactions, it is important to distinguish between a simple misunderstanding and a pattern of disrespect. While some people may inadvertently cross a line out of habit, manipulative behaviors like guilt-tripping or gaslighting are serious red flags that signal a breach of your fundamental safety. Consistently disregarding your requests for privacy or emotional space is not a minor oversight; it is a sign that the integrity of the relationship is at risk. Identifying these patterns early allows you to take corrective action before your sense of self is eroded.

When trust feels shaken, a calm and direct conversation can help you find your way back to a place of security. This involves sharing what feels "off" and listening to the other person, even when the topic is difficult. Repair is a deliberate process that requires patience and a shared commitment to rebuilding safety. By focusing on consideration and mutual care, you allow the relationship to remain resilient and adaptable as both of you change.

If you find yourself struggling to articulate your needs, try this short reflection:

- In which areas of my life do I feel most protective of my space?

- What specific physical or emotional signals tell me a line has been crossed?

- How can I express these needs from a place of clarity rather than frustration?

Putting these thoughts into words helps you move toward a more intentional way of relating to others. It ensures that your boundaries serve as a bridge to deeper connection rather than a barrier.

Physical and Material Boundaries: Recognizing Personal Space

Physical boundaries are the primary way you protect your comfort and sense of safety. They allow you to feel steady in crowded public spaces and intimate relationships alike. Whether you are requesting more room in a busy hallway or choosing a handshake over a hug, these choices are essential for your peace of mind. When someone stands too close and you feel your shoulders tighten, your body is providing an immediate signal that your physical space has been compromised. Acknowledging and honoring these signals keeps your daily interactions grounded in a sense of personal security.

Material boundaries involve your belongings, your finances, and how you choose to share them. These standards draw a clear line around your resources, defining the terms under which you are willing to be generous. For instance, you may be happy to lend a favorite book but prefer that others not use your personal laptop. In shared living situations, setting clear expectations regarding bills and shared items is imperative. Establishing these systems early prevents the build-up of tension and ensures that everyone involved feels a sense of fairness and respect.

Communicating these standards works best when you are direct, yet composed. If someone borrows a possession without asking, a calm statement such as, "I would prefer you check with me before using my things," sets a firm limit. If the behavior continues, a direct reminder reinforces your needs without escalating into a conflict. By being consistent, you teach others how to interact with your world in a way that feels respectful to you.

Even with clear communication, you may encounter pushback, especially when long-standing habits are involved. While it is helpful to understand the other person's perspective, it is more important to stay firm regarding what matters to your well-being. In practical terms, this might involve:

- Agreeing on a pre-set system for shared expenses so no one feels taken advantage of.

- Clearly defining which areas of a home are private versus which are common spaces.

- Maintaining a mental or physical list of personal items that are simply off-limits for lending.

If challenges around your physical or material space continue to resurface, take a moment to reflect on why these specific lines feel so significant. Ask yourself:

- Which specific possessions or spaces feel most tied to my sense of peace?

- How does my body react when these lines are crossed?

- What language allows me to explain my needs from a place of clarity rather than irritation?

Writing these thoughts down clarifies your needs for yourself first, making it easier to share them with others. Over time, being steady and open in these conversations creates an environment where your space and belongings are acknowledged as extensions of your personal integrity.

Sexual Boundaries: Understanding and Communicating Consent

Sexual boundaries are a vital aspect of personal safety and mutual understanding in intimate relationships. Knowing your limits and expressing them clearly allows you to protect your peace and ensures that your well-being remains a priority. These boundaries define your comfort levels and provide a foundation for interactions that are respectful and safe. Recognizing your own limits requires a deep understanding of your comfort regarding physical affection. This self-awareness allows you to express your needs with clarity, ensuring that your boundaries are honored by your partners. Effectively communicating these limits relies on both verbal and non-verbal cues, which are essential for maintaining a culture of consent.

Consent is the element that gives sexual boundaries their true meaning. It requires a clear, willing, and ongoing agreement from everyone involved. Consent must be explicit, mutual, and granted freely without any sense of pressure. In any intimate moment, it is important to remember that consent can be withdrawn at any time. Your personal guidelines may shift as you grow and change, and that is a natural part of staying present with a partner. Prioritizing enthusiastic consent creates an environment where each person feels secure and valued, allowing for a deeper and more genuine connection.

Establishing these boundaries requires honest and ongoing dialogue. Using straightforward language to convey your needs prevents the misunderstandings that arise from unspoken expectations. As trust grows within a relationship, these conversations become a natural way to maintain closeness. By putting consent and communication first, you create a space where both people can speak openly and feel heard.

Digital Boundaries: Navigating Online Interactions

In an interconnected landscape, digital boundaries have become a primary tool for protecting your mental well-being. They act as a filter that safeguards your privacy and prevents the overwhelming expanse of the internet from encroaching on your personal peace.

With the pervasive influence of social media, maintaining these limits ensures that your online presence remains intentional and secure. Just as you protect your physical space, digital boundaries preserve your mental energy by preventing a constant flood of information from becoming a source of stress.

Staying mindful of your online limits is essential for protecting your sense of self. Boundary breaches can manifest as oversharing, which often jeopardizes personal security and invites unwelcome scrutiny. It is important to discern which parts of your life should remain private and which are suitable for public view. To build more resilient digital boundaries, you might:

- Manage your social media presence by focusing only on what feels true to your values.

- Curate your digital circles to include only those you truly trust.

- Adjust your privacy settings to control the flow of your personal information.

- Choose specific windows of time to check messages to prevent digital fatigue.

These small choices create the breathing room necessary to move through the online world with intention. Balancing digital engagement with your offline life is a distinctive challenge that requires you to prioritize real-world experiences. Strategies such as designated tech-free times allow you to set aside devices and focus on the present moment. This practice nurtures authentic relationships and helps you maintain an equilibrium between your virtual and tangible realities.

As we wrap up this chapter, remember that boundaries touch every part of your life. They help you move through the world with a sense of honesty, thoughtfulness, and self-respect. In the next section, we will look at how to know when it is time to be flexible, when it is time to hold steady, and how to keep your personal guidelines working for you as your life continues to change.

PART 4

WHEN TO STAND FIRM & WHEN TO FLEX

CHAPTER 5

FLEXIBILITY VS. FIRMNESS

Once you begin practicing boundaries in real life, you quickly discover that no two situations feel the same. Sometimes a clear line protects your peace. Other times, connection requires a little more nuance, timing, or grace. This chapter explores that tension, so you can stay true to yourself without becoming rigid, and stay open-hearted without abandoning your needs.

Recognizing When Boundaries Are Tested

You're at a family gathering, laughter all around and plates being passed, when someone starts asking questions that feel too close. You look away, try to change the subject, but they keep pressing. It can catch you off guard, especially when the person seems harmless or insists they're *just curious*. Becoming aware of these triggers matters, as they tend to repeat, whether through probing questions or unsolicited advice. These individuals might approach with a friendly facade, but their actions challenge your comfort zone, demanding your attention. Take note of the environment as well. Busy, chaotic settings often magnify these challenges, making it harder to stay attuned to your own needs. Catching these signs early helps you protect your peace before tension builds up.

It's helpful to think about the context, too. Sometimes a gentle reminder is enough, and other times you might need to stand firm. Think back and ask yourself: *Has this happened before? Is this a recurring pattern, or a one-time oversight?* The answer can help you choose whether to let something slide or set a clear limit. Your own physical feelings are often the best signal that a line is being stretched. You might notice your shoulders tensing or your mind racing for an exit. Paying attention to those reactions without judgment helps you see where your limits really lie. It can also be beneficial to consider the other person's perspective, whether they are acting out of stress or simply habits they haven't questioned yet. It can be stress, worry, or habits they haven't questioned yet. That doesn't excuse the behavior, but it can guide how you respond.

In the moment, practices like pausing to breathe, grounding your feet, or silently naming what you feel can provide the clarity you need to stay centered. Taking time later to explore these moments can deepen your awareness. Notice when and how your boundaries were tested and how you felt in response. You could ask yourself:

- What was I feeling when that question or comment landed?

- How did I respond in that moment?

- What do I wish I had done differently?

Looking back, you may start to notice patterns involving certain topics or people that unsettle you more often. These insights help you plan ahead, so drawing personal lines feels less like a reaction and more like a proactive part of how you care for yourself.

Step Into Your Boundary

Take a few minutes to connect with your personal guidelines through movement. This exercise helps you embody your limits, making your boundaries feel real and supported in both body and mind.

1. **Find a clear space** where you can stand and move comfortably.

2. **Physically walk a line** or stand tall in one spot. As you do, silently or aloud, state a boundary you want to honor, such as, "I need time to recharge," or, "I say no when my plate is full."

3. **Notice how your body feels** as you claim this space. Are you grounded? Tense? Confident?

4. **Repeat this with several different boundaries,** letting your posture and steps reinforce each one.

Afterward, ponder what felt natural and what felt challenging. Consider one small action you can take this week to honor the need that felt the hardest to hold. This is a gentle way to practice saying yes to your own needs.

Building Emotional Resilience to Strengthen Boundaries

Emotional resilience might be the cornerstone you didn't realize was needed for setting and maintaining limitations. It operates as an internal anchor, protecting you from the weight of guilt and fear when you value your own needs. With emotional resilience, you're less susceptible to crumbling under external pressures, whether they stem from a demanding boss or a well-meaning but overstepping friend. This resilience acts like a buffer, absorbing the emotional toll that honoring your own needs can sometimes incur, thereby reducing emotional exhaustion and preserving your stamina to stand firm.

Building emotional resilience goes beyond simply toughening up. It's about cultivating inner strength that resists the tendency toward self-sacrifice and guilt. Strengthening your emotional core equips you to withstand pushback and prevents you from internalizing shame. Staying centered in such instances is achievable by honing emotional regulation skills. Techniques like grounding exercises and controlled breathwork can soothe nerves during challenging conversations. Taking a slow, deep breath and noticing your feet steady on the ground can help you stay calm and centered in the moment.

As you gradually master the art of resilience, your confidence will naturally expand. Learning to trust yourself leads to growing self-assurance, reducing lingering doubts about your decisions. These small victories serve as a foundation for enduring confidence that becomes an anchor over time, ready to guide you through more significant challenges with a steady hand. It is beneficial to celebrate these milestones by acknowledging the hard work and growth involved in building this inner strength and resilience.

Cultivating emotional detachment must not be mistaken for shutting down emotionally. It's about maintaining equilibrium in the face of criticism or disapproval and creating a new emotional perspective. Shifting your mindset aids this process. It involves perceiving negative feedback as information and data points rather than personal failings. This healthy perspective safeguards self-respect while you enforce limits, distinguishing it from avoidance, which tends toward emotional isolation. By viewing setbacks as learning opportunities, you nurture a resilient mindset.

Surround yourself with individuals who value your space, and your emotional resilience will strengthen. Identifying energy-draining relationships is important, as is discerning when they need revisiting. A robust support system, whether through accountability partners, mentors or trusted peers, bolsters your confidence. These relationships provide reassurance and perspective, allowing you to defend your boundaries with resolve and ease. Finding a community of like-minded individuals who share your commitment to self-care and healthy practices can significantly enhance your journey.

Overcoming Guilt, Fear, and Anxiety in Boundary-Setting

Facing guilt and fear when defining personal guidelines can feel like wrestling something you can't quite see, but it's part of the process of protecting what matters to you. Guilt often whispers that taking a stand for yourself is selfish, a narrative that usually roots itself in familial or cultural traditions where advocating for yourself was not supported. Understanding the origin of these feelings aids in confronting them directly. Moreover, the fear of conflict and rejection can immobilize action. You're not alone in fearing that setting limits might invite judgment or isolation. Building your tolerance for these feelings through small, gradual steps makes you more comfortable and equipped to manage potential outcomes. Affirmations, reminding yourself that your needs are valid, become vital tools in this journey.

Reframing your perception of guilt and fear can noticeably change the narrative. It is helpful to recognize the difference between a healthy sense of responsibility toward others and the unhealthy guilt that acts as a source of unnecessary self-doubt. Learn to view fear as an indicator of potential growth rather than a formidable barrier. When you feel that spark of anxiety, recognize it as a sign that you are expanding your comfort zone and reclaiming your agency. Engaging in visualization exercises helps build confidence, allowing you to rehearse successfully communicating your needs with a sense of calm. Similarly, practicing these scenarios in your mind or a safe space readies you for real-life interactions, enhancing your resilience and decreasing self-criticism.

Empowerment through self-advocacy transforms your internal landscape. As you set each guideline, your self-worth becomes more firmly rooted, establishing your own authority in decision-making. A sense of certainty gradually replaces hesitation, guiding your choices with confidence instead of doubt. This transformation unfolds slowly, making it important to recognize and appreciate the small victories along the way. Each reinforcement nurtures your ability to maintain firm and healthy practices, bolstering inner strength. Your empowerment acts as a beacon, not only for yourself but also inspiring those around you to honor their own needs and limits.

Cultivating emotional resilience equips you to meet internal challenges with wisdom and grace. By developing a resilient mindset, you focus on growth rather than perceived setbacks. While much of this work happens within, your support system acts as a reliable resource during this process. Surrounding yourself with people who value your boundaries provides encouragement when self-doubt emerges. Reinforcement from these allies strengthens your commitment to your personal limits and builds your inner resolve. As your resilience develops, you will become more adept at discerning the difference between helpful feedback and unnecessary criticism.

Handling Pushback: Strategies for Graceful Conflict Resolution

Pushback can emerge unexpectedly, sometimes masquerading as well-intentioned advice or concern that camouflages with underlying criticism. Recognizing these tactics is the first step toward responding with confidence. An individual might attempt to guilt-trip you by implying your boundaries are selfish, or they could cloak their disapproval in "care," making it more challenging to identify. This recognition equips you to respond effectively, allowing you to maintain your composure and inner strength without losing your ground. Embracing these interactions as learning opportunities can turn perceived obstacles into sources of personal power.

Stand firm and respond with clarity when confronted with pushback. Using "I" statements allows you to claim your feelings and needs with ownership. For instance, you might say, "I appreciate your concern, but this decision is what is best for my well-being." Such responses keep the focus on respectful dialogue, ensuring your personal guidelines remain intact while transforming potentially tense situations into opportunities for honest conversation.

Consistency is the primary tool for deterring future challenges. When others observe you standing firm repeatedly, they learn to see and value your limits. Techniques like calmly reiterating your needs emphasize their importance and help reset the expectations of those around you. Phrases such as, "I have already explained my position on this," serve to minimize resistance over time. This steadfastness communicates that your needs are non-negotiable, which eventually diminishes the frequency of repeated challenges. Practicing this consistency across different areas of your life reinforces your authority and helps you uphold your standards with ease.

Constructing confidence in how you protect your space transforms hesitation into resolve. Rehearsing these situations through mental practice or role-playing enhances your readiness for real-life encounters. These exercises offer safe spaces to build self-assurance and reveal areas where you may want to refine your approach. Meanwhile, activities like reflective journaling help you celebrate your successes and pinpoint specific growth opportunities. Affirmations, such as, "My needs are valid, and I have the right to protect them," reinforce this mindset, empowering you to maintain your limits without second-guessing yourself.

When to Stand Firm & Reinforce Boundaries

Standing firm begins with viewing your own clarity not as aggression, but as a fundamental act of self-respect. It serves as a reminder to both yourself and others that your needs are valid. Knowing what truly matters to you makes it easier to hold your ground, as your personal values work like a quiet compass, guiding you through moments when you might feel tempted to waver.

* Small, practical steps can help you stay steady in the moment:

* Maintain an open posture. Standing tall helps you project a quiet confidence that your body registers as safety.

* Hold steady eye contact. This ensures your words feel grounded and direct.

* Use calm, measured speech. Speaking clearly signals cer-

tainty without the need to raise your voice.

- Plan for common challenges. Anticipating situations that test your limits allows you to respond intentionally rather than reacting out of stress.

- Set clear intentions. Decide ahead of time what you will say or do if a specific line is crossed.

Developing a personalized action plan can bring your focus into even sharper relief. Start by identifying the specific areas where you feel your limits are currently blurred. For instance, if work-life balance is a concern, your plan might include specific actions like closing your email at a set time or delegating tasks that fall outside your role. By tailoring these strategies to fit the different contexts of your life, whether at home, work, or in social circles, you ensure that your approach remains realistic and sustainable.

Ongoing awareness is what keeps these efforts alive. Regularly assessing your experiences helps you recognize what worked well and where a different approach might be necessary. Reflective questions can guide this growth:

- What did I learn about my own capacity during this experience?

- How can I refine my communication to feel even more grounded next time?

- Did I stay true to my core principles, even if the situation was difficult?

Adapting your strategies based on these honest self-checks builds a deep sense of resilience. Over time, this practice ensures that each new situation feels less like a high-stakes test and more like an opportunity to show up for yourself with integrity and quiet confidence.

When to Remain Flexible & Adapt Boundaries

Life is a constant state of change, and the boundaries you need will evolve along with it. Staying open to adjusting your limits helps you protect what matters most as you grow. Adaptability does not mean sacrificing your core values; rather, it reflects your capacity to respond with wisdom to life's transitions. Consider a career shift, where a new role may require a temporary re-evaluation of your work-life limits. Similarly, shifts in family dynamics, such as the arrival of a new family member or becoming a caregiver, often call for a fresh perspective. Adaptability in these moments ensures your boundaries support your growth rather than hindering it.

Recognizing when to adapt requires a sensitivity to your current environment. Moving to a new city or country might introduce different cultural norms that challenge your established expectations. Entering or leaving relationships also demands a thoughtful reconfiguration. A new partnership requires fresh limits that safeguard your individuality while honoring the emerging connection. Conversely, exiting a relationship may require more robust standards as you work to reclaim your personal space and autonomy.

Adapting your personal limits can begin with establishing "trial boundaries" during significant transitions. This strategy allows you to test a new arrangement without making a permanent commitment. For instance, if you assume additional responsibilities at work, temporarily adjusting your availability can help you balance expectations while you assess your actual capacity. Reassessing your priorities in unfamiliar terrain allows you to preserve your core values while adopting the flexibility needed to navigate new professional or personal commitments.

Understanding the necessity of adaptability ensures that your boundaries serve a supportive, rather than restrictive, function. It requires a delicate equilibrium to prevent flexibility from slipping into self-sacrifice. This balance acknowledges that while personal guidelines are vital, they should grow and evolve alongside you to reflect the dynamic nature of your life. Maintaining this balance with integrity means staying true to your non-negotiables while permitting yourself the room to transform and grow.

Adapting Boundaries with Integrity

As your life shifts, so can your boundaries. This evolution is a natural part of growing into your most authentic self. Whether you are facing a new job with different hours or a shift in family responsibilities, remaining flexible while maintaining your integrity is vital. Rigid standards can sometimes lead to unintended isolation, making it difficult to engage meaningfully with the world. By staying adaptable, you allow for growth and transformation, ensuring your personal guidelines address your current needs as well as your future aspirations. Flexibility grounded in self-respect allows you to adjust without losing sight of who you are becoming.

When evaluating whether to change a boundary, start with quiet introspection. Contemplate whether a potential adjustment feels aligned with your core values or if it feels more like self-sacrifice. Evaluate how this flexibility impacts your daily well-being and your relationships, remaining mindful of those moments when being "easygoing" might edge into compromising your fundamental needs. Understanding this distinction protects you against patterns of self-neglect. The goal is to keep your values closely aligned with how you respond to the realities of your life. Healthy boundaries are not static lines but living agreements that reflect your growth, your self-awareness, and your evolving understanding of what you need to thrive.

Adapting a boundary does not mean you have failed to uphold it. Rather, it signals that you are paying attention. Life will ask different things of you in different seasons, and wisdom lies in knowing when reinforcement is necessary and when thoughtful recalibration will better serve your well-being. When your adjustments are rooted in clarity instead of pressure, flexibility becomes a form of strength rather than surrender.

To adapt without compromising yourself, try following a simple framework:

- **Assess the impact.** Consider how the change affects your long-term goals and your emotional health.

- **Determine the direction.** Does this adjustment facilitate your growth, or does it feel like a step backward?

- **Consult trusted allies.** Speak with people who understand your values and can offer a fresh perspective when you feel uncertain.

- **Implement gradual changes.** Avoid sweeping alterations; instead, take small steps to ensure each shift feels right before moving forward.

As you adapt, maintaining your inner compass ensures your boundaries continue to complement who you are. With practice, you will find that your personal guidelines can be both robust and adaptable, offering a firm yet flexible foundation for your personal development.

As we close this chapter, keep in mind that your needs are allowed to change as you grow. In the next part of our journey, we will explore how to build these guidelines from the ground up, ensuring they feel real, flexible, and deeply rooted in your true self.

PART 5

HOW TO CREATE BOUNDARIES

CHAPTER 6

THE BOUNDARY CREATION FRAMEWORK

Understanding boundaries is one thing. Creating them in your real life is another. Many people can recognize when a line has been crossed but still struggle to define what that line should actually look like. This chapter introduces a simple framework to help you turn awareness into clear, intentional boundaries that reflect your values and protect your energy.

Decision Framework for Boundary-Setting

Setting personal standards can feel daunting, especially if you have spent years putting the needs of everyone else first. To move forward, it helps to have a clear, step-by-step method to guide your choices so they feel true to your identity and your core values.

This decision framework offers a practical path to help you create and maintain guidelines that protect your time, energy, and peace of mind. Here is what you will explore:

- **Step 1: Internal Readiness.** Notice where you feel stretched thin and identify the subconscious blocks that prevent you from drawing new lines.

- **Step 2: Boundary Design.** Translate your needs into fair, kind, and sustainable limits.

- **Step 3: Emotional Intelligence.** Learn to sense when a line is being tested and develop the resilience to respond calmly.

- **Step 4: Boundary Mastery.** Build the habits necessary to adjust your boundaries as life changes without losing sight of your principles.

Each step builds upon the last, helping you move from simply knowing your limits to living them out in your everyday life. This framework serves as your compass on the journey to reclaim your personal sovereignty. By following these steps, you can pursue both personal fulfillment and respectful, honest relationships with the people around you.

Step 1: Internal Readiness

Before you start setting new standards, it helps to get honest about what's happening inside: what feels stretched, what feels steady, and what truly matters to you. Many of us harbor subconscious roadblocks that hinder us from standing up for ourselves. These can come from the fear of disappointing others, guilt over saying no, or an ingrained tendency to please. The first step is simply seeing what stands in your way. When you acknowledge these ingrained patterns, you begin to dismantle them. It's common for empaths and people pleasers to struggle with this phase due to their heightened sensitivity to others' emotions and needs.

Overcoming these hurdles requires a shift in mindset. You might feel guilt or fear, worrying that asserting yourself will alienate others or disrupt the precious harmony you've worked hard to maintain. It's important to remember that setting limits is a tool for balance rather than an obstacle to closeness. Boundaries are bridges to healthier interactions and less stressful engagements. Reframing guilt as a natural response rather than a verdict on your character can be liberating. Prioritizing yourself is not selfish; it is necessary for growing sustainable relationships and personal development.

To support this new perspective, you can begin to build a mindset that favors self-compassion over self-sacrifice. Some people find it helpful to experiment with small mindset shifts, such as reminding themselves, "I am worthy of setting limits," or "My needs are important." Simple reframes like these can begin loosening the old beliefs that keep boundaries out of reach. These mantras help reinforce your right to self-care and autonomy. Additionally, engaging in self-reflection can help you better live in accordance with your values and bolster your confidence in asserting them.

This shift in internal readiness is exactly what transformed the experience of Laura, a graphic designer who often stretched herself too thin at work. When burnout finally caught up with her, she took time to look honestly at her fear of rejection and failure. By addressing those internal drivers, she began to set gentler limits with clients and colleagues. Over time, this made her work more focused and left her with more energy for life outside the office. Laura's story shows how getting real about what drives us inside can help us make the small, deliberate choices that change how we show up every day.

Step 2: Boundary Design

Now it's time to identify where limitations are needed. Begin by assessing areas in your life where you feel drained or resentful. These emotions often signal a breach in personal space and deserve your immediate attention. Whether it's an overbearing colleague or a friend who consistently oversteps, pinpointing these areas helps you prioritize which lines were crossed and need attention first.

Once you have identified these points of tension, you can begin to turn them into clear, actionable boundaries. This involves articulating your needs in specific terms rather than vague requests. For example, instead of saying, "I need more space," try, "I need two hours of uninterrupted time each evening to focus on myself." Expressing yourself clearly ensures both you and those around you understand the expectation and its purpose, providing a mutual ground for understanding each other's space.

Making your limits understood depends on confident expression. Assertive communication involves expressing your needs clearly and respectfully while honoring the rights of others. This approach allows you to use "I" statements to own your feelings and needs, such as, "I feel overwhelmed when I am interrupted during work hours." Practicing these statements can ease anxiety and promote a more confident delivery when the moment arises.

Writing out what you might say in challenging moments can give you the additional confidence needed to hold your ground. For instance, if a friend frequently drops by unannounced, a script might sound like: "I value our time together, but I need a heads-up before visits to ensure I can give you my full attention." Scripts like these prepare you for common breaches, allowing for smooth, unflustered conversation. Additionally, these scripts can serve as a foundational tool for maintaining consistency in messages without being caught off guard.

Step 3: Emotional Intelligence

Emotional intelligence is the backbone of successful boundary management. It involves strengthening self-trust and emotional resilience. These are qualities that enable you to handle defining personal guidelines with grace and effectiveness. Trusting yourself means believing in your ability to make decisions that honor your values without second-guessing or faltering. Emotional resilience equips you to bounce back from setbacks and stay grounded in your needs, even when facing external pressures.

Paying attention to your emotions before, during, and after you set a boundary helps you stay steady and respond in ways that feel authentic. It is helpful to anticipate emotional reactions like anxiety or fear when you begin emphasizing your limits. In these moments, use techniques such as deep breathing or visualization to maintain your calm. After drawing your personal lines, reflect on the experience. Notice what went well and what could be improved. This reflection enhances your self-awareness and prepares you for future interactions, turning previous challenges into valuable learning experiences.

Conflict resolution skills are indispensable when facing pushback. Developing these skills involves learning how to navigate disagreements without compromising your boundaries or resorting to defensiveness. It's about maintaining composure and seeking understanding rather than victory. When you face conflict with both empathy and steadiness, it opens the door for honest conversations that can bring you closer and build real trust.

Consider the experience of Alex, a teacher who noticed work emails were regularly intruding upon his personal time on week-ends. Rather than allowing resentment toward the school administration to build, Alex paused to reflect on his own habits. He realized that by reflexively checking notifications, he was choosing to remain "on the clock" even when it wasn't required.

Using this insight, Alex decided to take ownership of his digital space. He established a personal rule to silence work notifications on Friday evenings and communicated this change proactively. Alex explained to his supervisor, "To ensure I'm fully recharged and present for my students on Monday, I've decided to step away from work emails over the weekend." This approach did more than just protect Alex's personal time; it demonstrated professional maturity and a commitment to long-term performance. By taking accountability for his own accessibility, Alex modeled a sustainable work-life balance that commanded respect without requiring others to change their behavior.

Step 4: Boundary Mastery

Maintaining boundaries over time requires both vigilance and commitment. Consistently upholding your standards, even when it feels awkward, reminds both you and those around you why they matter. This consistency creates a new norm where your needs are respected as much as the needs of others. When violations occur, addressing them promptly prevents trust from eroding and ensures your expectations remain intact, preserving the integrity and balance of your relationships.

Recovering after a setback involves an honest conversation with yourself about what went wrong and how it can be avoided in the future. This might mean revisiting a situation where your personal lines were ignored or misunderstood and reaffirming their importance. Patience is essential during this process: both for yourself as you learn from experience and for others as they adjust to your new limits. By demonstrating this patience, you provide the necessary space for meaningful growth and long-term adaptation.

To sustain these limits over the long term, you must find a middle ground between empathy and firmness. This balance allows you to keep your relationships strong while still honoring your own needs. It is about understanding the perspectives of others without compromising your own well-being. This equilibrium prevents flexibility from slipping into self-sacrifice and fosters a culture of mutual cooperation. By practicing empathy while expressing yourself confidently, you create an environment where all parties feel valued, ultimately strengthening trust.

In the long run, honoring your needs gently but firmly helps you feel calmer, more connected to others, and more at peace with yourself. Individuals who maintain clear boundaries often experience higher levels of self-esteem, a stronger sense of direction, and enhanced life satisfaction. This mastery allows you to navigate life's challenges with greater confidence and serenity, knowing that your personal foundation is secure.

Clarifying Your Values Through Boundaries

Use this exercise to visualize how your guidelines honor what matters most to you. Seeing your needs and boundaries side by side turns abstract awareness into practical steps.

The Values-Alignment Map:

1. **Identify your Core Values.** Draw a T chart. On the left side of a page, list the values or needs that sustain you, such as rest, focus, connection, or creativity.

2. **Define the Protection.** On the right side, write a specific boundary that protects or supports each value. For example, if "rest" is a core value, your boundary might be

"silencing all work notifications after 7:00 p.m."

3. **Assess the Alignment.** Look at your map and ask your-self: How does each boundary help me live in accordance with my values? Which ones feel natural to uphold, and which require more intentional effort?

4. **Commit to One Action.** Choose one small step this week to strengthen a boundary that feels important but challenging.

Seeing your needs and boundaries side by side turns awareness into practical steps you can take. This exercise shows that personal guidelines aren't restrictions; they are ways of honoring your needs and living in alignment with what truly matters. Treat this as a promise to yourself: to care for your own needs while staying open to meaningful connection.

This framework isn't just a set of steps. It's an ongoing practice of self-care. Each choice you make to prioritize your own needs shapes a life that feels more balanced, genuine, and joyful. Let this be your gentle guide as you keep growing into the life you truly want.

As we conclude this chapter, remember that boundary-setting is not merely about rules; it is about living in a way that feels honest and feels true to who you are.

In the next chapter, we'll look inward and see what it really takes to get ready to set boundaries that stick by digging in on *Step 1.* We will focus on building deep internal readiness by understanding your fears and what truly matters most, ensuring the standards you create feel steady and entirely your own.

CHAPTER 7

STEP 1: INTERNAL READINESS

Before a boundary can be spoken aloud, something quieter has to shift within you. The beliefs you carry about responsibility, harmony, and your role in other people's lives often determine what you allow long before a situation even arises. Internal readiness begins with noticing those patterns and deciding which ones still serve the person you are becoming.

Overcoming Internal Barriers

You're at a dinner table, heart pounding, rehearsing how to say *no* to another request. All around you, the room hums with conversation, yet inside, you're caught wrestling the fear of letting someone down. That fear of conflict, rejection, or criticism can run deep, especially if you've spent years putting others first. Often, it stems from earlier moments when speaking up led to pain or disapproval, leaving a mark that still shapes your choices today.

When fear becomes the compass, it steers you away from what you truly want and closer to what others expect. Over time, life can start to feel unfamiliar, almost as if you're living someone else's story. This split between who you are and who you feel you should be can weigh heavily, adding quiet tension that grows until it's hard to ignore.

Low self-esteem and the urge to please often go hand in hand, creating a cycle that is difficult to break. When your sense of worth is tied to keeping others happy, it can feel safer to say *yes* than risk disapproval. Yet constantly chasing acceptance leaves you drained and disconnected from your own needs. Recognizing how these patterns formed and the quiet beliefs that hold them in place is the first step toward change.

Another obstacle is the belief that setting boundaries makes you selfish. Maybe you've heard that caring for yourself is wrong, or that it means turning your back on loved ones. Over time, these messages can settle in as quiet truths, making guilt feel inevitable when you try to speak up. Reflecting on when this guilt surfaces and where those beliefs came from can help you see them for what they are, echoes of the past, which have nothing to do with who you are today.

One way to start is by gently examining the moments that feel hardest. Ask yourself:

- *What specific situations spark my fear of rejection?*

- *How do my past experiences shape my responses in the present?*

Noticing the answers helps reveal the invisible barriers that have guided your choices. By naming them, you begin to loosen their hold, giving yourself space to choose differently next time.

Change often starts quietly, with a simple awareness: you have the right to honor your needs. And with each small step, the path to self-care becomes clearer and more your own.

Mapping Your Triggers and Responses

Use this exercise to uncover patterns that make setting personal guidelines feel intimidating and practice choosing new, empowered responses:

1. **Identify your triggers.** List situations where you often feel anxious, guilty, or hesitant about asserting a limit.

2. **Map the typical response.** For each trigger, write down what you usually do or say and how that choice makes you feel afterward.

3. **Draft an alternative.** Describe a response that honors your needs while still respecting the other person. Write this next to your usual reaction.

4. **Analyze the gap.** Consider the differences between your old response and the new choice. What feels possible? What feels challenging?

5. **Practice one shift.** Pick one trigger to focus on this week. Practice responding with your new approach and notice any shift in your confidence.

This approach helps you see recurring patterns, understand the fears behind them, and create concrete strategies to act differently. By practicing in a safe, structured way, you move from reacting out of fear to responding with intention, strengthening your ability to protect your time, energy, and well-being.

Clarity as a Catalyst

Identifying personal roadblocks is not about dwelling on past mistakes but about understanding them as stepping stones for growth. By pinpointing them, you can see where change is needed, creating a roadmap for your personal evolution. This journey requires courage and honesty: qualities you already possess in abundance. As you explore these aspects of yourself, remember that each insight brings you closer to a life where your needs are valued. This newfound understanding emboldens you to nurture better relationships that thrive on mutual regard and open dialogue.

With this fresh awareness, you can start crafting strategies that align with your genuine self. This might mean setting small, manageable goals for reinforcing boundaries in low-stakes situations. For instance, practice saying "no" politely when a request clashes with your priorities, or take a moment to assess your capacity before agreeing to new commitments. The key is to build confidence incrementally, celebrating each success along the way. These successes, though small, are monumental in breaking the cycle of self-neglect. The more you practice, the more natural it will feel to express your needs without guilt or fear.

While you continue this introspective work, be gentle with yourself. Change takes time, and it's normal to stumble along the way. View these stumbles as part of the learning process. Continue moving forward, knowing that each step brings you closer to a life where you are empowered to express yourself fully and sincerely.

Reframing Beliefs Around Boundaries

Boundaries often carry an undeserved reputation. They're often unfairly viewed as shutting people out rather than making room for healthier bonds. However, it's time to challenge these limiting beliefs and see them in a new light. They are not acts of selfishness; they are genuine expressions of self-care. Think of them as the invisible lines that define how you wish to interact with the world.

By defining clear guidelines, you solidify your right to personal space and emotional freedom. This isn't about shutting people out. It's about protecting your well-being while inviting healthier interactions. When you reframe them as acts of self-care, you empower yourself to maintain balance and integrity.

Guilt often intertwines with assertiveness, discouraging you from voicing your needs. In many cultures, speaking up can be seen as defiance or disrespect, and this guilt becomes a heavy weight. However, standing up for yourself isn't aggression or selfishness. It's a form of clear self-assurance. Consider:

- How does guilt influence the way I express your needs?

- What cultural messages shaped my view of confidence?

- When have I felt that speaking up meant harming someone else?

Exploring these questions helps you recognize that taking care of your needs is *necessary* for mental and emotional well-being, not a betrayal of kindness.

Societal norms also play a role in shaping how you perceive assertiveness. Many of these norms discourage speaking up, especially for those who naturally prioritize the comfort of others. These individuals often feel compelled to put others' needs first, creating a cycle that sacrifices their own well-being. Challenging these norms requires courage and a willingness to redefine what it means to embrace personal agency. It involves recognizing that your voice deserves to be heard and that setting limits is a healthy practice, not a societal faux pas. By viewing self-expression as a form of self-care rather than rebellion, you open the door to more balanced and honest interactions.

Normalizing standing up for yourself starts by seeing it as a method of sharing your thoughts and needs openly and thoughtfully while remaining considerate of others' feelings. Striking this balance will help particularly in relationships where honest dialogue nurtures trust and shared understanding. When you replace guilt with grounded self-ownership, you acknowledge that your needs are just as important as anyone else's. This shift in perspective allows you to communicate more effectively, reducing misunderstandings and fostering healthier connections.

When it comes to speaking your truth, replacing guilt with self-ownership transforms your interactions. This transformation isn't about dismissing others. It's about standing firm in your needs while acknowledging theirs. You learn to take responsibility for your feelings and actions, understanding that they are valid expressions of who you are. This sense of ownership empowers you to protect your space confidently, knowing that doing so enriches your relationships rather than hinders them. And like all skills, this blooms with practice, each encounter a stepping stone toward confidence in articulating your needs.

As you embrace this new perspective, remember that it's a skill that improves with practice. Each interaction offers an opportunity to refine how you communicate your needs, presenting a challenge to wield your voice with compassion. Start small by setting boundaries in low-stakes situations, gradually building confidence in more significant interactions. Over time, trusting your voice becomes second nature. It becomes a natural extension of your true self.

By challenging limiting beliefs and embracing confident self-expression, you pave the way for more fulfilling relationships and a stronger sense of self. It's about reclaiming your narrative and redefining how you engage with the world around you. Through this process, you discover that boundaries are not obstacles but pathways to a life to a life shaped by balance, self-trust, and meaningful relationships.

Standing up for yourself may feel uncomfortable initially, especially if you've internalized the belief that doing so is wrong. But with each step forward, you dismantle these outdated narratives and replace them with ones that celebrate self-care and empowerment. Embracing the discomfort as part of growth; it is an understanding that change often requires stepping out of familiar patterns.

As you work to reshape your beliefs about boundaries, patience plays a central role. Give yourself grace as you navigate this new terrain, acknowledging that progress may be gradual but no less meaningful. Celebrate each victory, no matter how small, recognizing that every step forward is a testament to your commitment to living authentically.

By reframing your approach to personal limits and self-assurance, you unlock the potential for

- Deeper, more fulfilling connections;

- Greater self-awareness and confidence; and

- A life where your needs are honored and respected.

This transformation unfolds not only in moments where you speak up but also in quiet reflections that strengthen your resolve. Trust the process. Over time, self-doubt can give way to self-assurance, helping you live with balance and courage.

Mindset Shifts for Guilt-Free Communication

Standing in a crowded room, your chest tightens as you brace yourself to say *no*. The guilt weighs heavy, as though speaking up somehow wrongs those around you. Many of us grew up equating speaking up and self-advocacy with defiance, shaped by messages suggesting that asking for what we need disrupts harmony. Yet at its core, clear communication shows both care for yourself and consideration for others. Over time, this reframing can soften the fear that your voice creates distance, helping you recognize that honesty often builds deeper, more sustainable connection.

To perceive this more readily, you must separate assertiveness from selfishness. The latter dismisses other people's needs entirely while the former, by contrast, honors your own needs while still recognizing those around you. This distinction clears a path toward communication that feels balanced rather than forceful.

Adopting a growth mindset can also help release guilt. Instead of viewing mistakes as failures, they become essential data points.. If you phrase something awkwardly or react too quickly, pause afterward and ask: *What might I try differently next time?* Each small lesson deepens your understanding of what matters most to you. With practice, what once felt uncomfortable begins to feel natural, allowing confidence to replace hesitation as you learn to trust your voice.

Setting realistic goals can transforms intention into practice:

* Say *no* to an extra task when your plate is already full.

* Carve out a few minutes of quiet after work instead of immediately answering messages.

* Gently express a preference instead of staying silent.

With each step, celebrate the progress itself rather than chasing flawless conversation. Perfection can keep you frozen. Progress keeps you moving. Over time, confidence grows naturally as speaking up becomes a familiar habit.

These mindset shifts (seeing speaking up as thoughtful, embracing mistakes as learning, and valuing steady progress) can ease guilt's hold. Gradually, conversations become less about proving your worth and more about sharing who you truly are.

As we close this chapter on internal readiness, remember: reframing assertiveness as an act of self-respect is what makes guilt-free connection possible. When you see it as a way to honor your own needs rather than a desire to overpower anyone else, you create a space for dialogue that feels genuine and balanced.

Welcoming mistakes as part of growth, setting small, manageable goals, and celebrating each bit of progress will gradually shift how you show up in your relationships. Over time, this builds the confidence to speak openly and to stand firm when it matters.

In the next chapter, we'll move from observation to action. We'll explore practical strategies for creating effective boundaries that align with your values and protect your well-being. Step by step, you'll shape a life where your voice feels at home. Stay curious about who you are becoming; this journey is about drawing clear lines, honoring your truth, and claiming a life that is unmistakably your own.

CHAPTER 8

STEP 2: BOUNDARY DESIGN

Recognizing that something needs to change is only the beginning. The next step is giving that insight a clear shape. A boundary becomes real when you define what you will allow, what you will decline, and how you will communicate that decision to others. Boundary design is the process of turning your values and needs into limits that are clear enough to guide your choices and steady enough to support your well-being.

Identifying and Defining Boundaries

Establishing personal guidelines begins with a clear-eyed assessment of where your energy is leaking. Identifying where limits are absent or weak is the primary requirement for reclaiming your peace of mind. To start, evaluate the specific areas of your life where you consistently feel overextended or burdened by resentment. The presence of resentment is your most reliable compass:

it signals that a boundary has been crossed or was never established in the first place.

Whether it is a stream of work emails invading your evenings or a social connection that monopolizes your time, these friction points indicate a need for reinforcement. Reexamine the situations where you feel taken for granted. By pinpointing these deficiencies, you can determine exactly where new standards will benefit you most, allowing you to move from a reactive state to one of intentionality.

Once you've identified these critical areas, differentiate clearly between essential and negotiable boundaries. Essential boundaries are nonnegotiables. They protect your core needs and intrinsic values. For example, maintaining a work-free zone after 7:00 p.m. to preserve family time might be an essential boundary. On the other hand, negotiable boundaries allow for some flexibility, such as occasionally staying late at work for an important project. Recognizing which of them fall into each category helps you allocate your energy wisely, thereby maintaining balance and promoting long-term well-being.

Prioritize and sort these limits into high- and low-priority categories. High-priority boundaries echo your core personal values and protect what matters most to you. For instance, if personal growth is a significant value, setting aside time each week for a hobby or study becomes a high-priority boundary. Low-priority boundaries might involve preferences that, while desirable, aren't fundamental to your well-being and could be adjusted as necessary.

Measure these carefully sorted personal rules against your core values, beliefs, desires and needs to ensure they genuinely support your life goals and aspirations. Consider what principles guide your decisions. Perhaps honesty, creativity, or family take precedence. By mirroring your guidelines with these values, you cultivate a life that shows who you truly are, not just who others expect you to be. This alignment provides a sense of authenticity and cohesion across different aspects of your life.

Daily Mini Steps

Strengthening your guidelines requires consistent, low-stakes practice to build confidence.

1. **Select one simple challenge** for the week: say "no" once per day, take a full lunch break, or turn off notifications immediately after work.

2. **Observe the experience.** Each day, notice how it feels to practice this step. Note what is easy and what feels uncomfortable.

3. **Reflect on the impact.** At the end of the week, consider how honoring this need affected your energy, focus, or sense of self-respect.

4. **Decide on the next step:** repeat the experiment, add a new boundary, or adjust your approach based on what you learned.

This practice helps you focus your boundary-setting where it counts most, ensuring your choices echo who you truly are. Revisit this exercise regularly as your life unfolds, refining your limits so they stay in tune with your evolving needs and aspirations.

As you move forward, remember that drawing personal lines is an ongoing process. As life evolves, so too will your needs and priorities. Regularly reassess your boundaries to ensure they continue to serve you effectively, allowing you to make adjustments as unexpected changes occur. This adaptability allows you to remain true to yourself while navigating life's ever-changing landscape. Keeping a conscious watch on your emotional and physical reactions can offer additional clues about when recalibration is necessary.

By taking these considered steps, you empower yourself to live authentically and fully, free from the weight of demands that don't honor your worth or needs. This empowerment extends beyond personal satisfaction, influencing other areas of your life by fostering healthier relationships, improved productivity, and a deeper sense of contentment and purpose.

Assertive Communication: Expressing Needs Clearly

You may find yourself at a crossroads, where the path to self-care meets the challenge of communicating your limits. This is where assertiveness becomes your trusted guide, offering guidance. At its core, it is about expressing your needs with confidence. It starts with the use of "I" statements, a simple yet powerful tool that shifts the focus from blame to personal experience. Instead of saying, "You always interrupt me," try, "I feel frustrated when I'm interrupted." This subtle shift reduces defensiveness and also opens the door for constructive dialogue and mutual understanding.

Your tone and body language are equally important. They convey their own message. Speak with calm and intention, using a steady voice that mirrors your inner conviction. Avoid crossing your arms or looking away, as these actions can signal discomfort or defensiveness. Instead, maintain eye contact and keep an open posture, inviting collaboration rather than confrontation. When you embody confidence through your tone, body language and overall presence, others are more likely to recognize your space and respond positively.

To communicate effectively, begin with a calm and steady state. This involves preparing yourself mentally before entering a conversation. Take a few deep breaths to center yourself, focusing on the message you want to convey rather than the emotions surrounding it. Approach the discussion with the intention to communicate and collaborate, not to confront. By doing so, you set the stage for a respectful exchange where both parties feel heard. Mindful preparation goes a long way in ensuring that you don't overwhelm yourself or the other person, keeping the dialogue constructive.

Establish expectations before tension turns into conflict. In new relationships, set boundaries early to prevent misunderstandings. In professional environments, vet the culture during the interview process to understand the team's communication norms and how urgent off-hours requests are handled. Understanding the operational rhythm in advance allows you to assess alignment with your values before you commit.

The same principle applies to your personal life. In a social context, you might clarify expectations with a friend who tends to call late at night: "I value our conversations, but I've realized I need to unplug after 9:00 p.m. to get enough sleep. I won't be answering calls after that time, but I'll catch up with you first thing in the morning." Setting these markers early prevents the slow build of resentment and ensures your relationships are built on mutual respect rather than silent endurance. Honest conversation is vital for maintaining healthy dynamics and avoiding the tension that arises from unvoiced concerns.

Scripts for Confident Expression

Using practical scripts supports you in articulating where you stand. Consider these examples as starting points to guide your own voice:

Professional Scenarios

- "I am currently at capacity with my current projects;

which of these should I deprioritize to make room for this new request?"

- "I want to give this my full attention, but I am offline after 6:00 p.m. I will provide a thorough update first thing tomorrow morning."

- "I appreciate your feedback; however, I need to process it before we discuss it further."

Personal and Social Scenarios

- "I value our time together, but I am not able to take on any more social commitments this weekend. Let's look at next month instead."

- "I'm uncomfortable with this topic and would prefer to move on to something else."

- "I need some quiet time after work to recharge, so I will join activities later."

These scripts serve as templates for expressing your needs without aggression or apology. They focus on your experience, which fosters understanding rather than defensiveness. By crafting personalized phrases that reflect your own voice, you enhance your ability to convey your limits while remaining approachable.

For those who struggle to find the right words in the moment, deliberate practice is essential. Role-playing scenarios with a trusted friend can bolster your confidence in delivering these responses naturally. Over time, expressing boundaries becomes second nature: it becomes a tool that allows you to navigate interactions with ease.

Remember that effective communication is a discipline refined over time. Be patient as you grow in this area, recognizing that it is an evolving process. Each conversation is an opportunity to strengthen your ability to speak with conviction, enhancing both your relationships and your sense of self-worth. As you refine these skills, you create an environment of mutual respect that encourages others to engage with you on similar terms.

Overcoming Communication Barriers

Have you ever stood on the threshold of an important conversation, only to feel your heart race as you sense it is time to set a boundary? You know what needs to be said, yet familiar doubts whisper for you to hold back. This hesitation is a universal experience when the moment calls for honest self-expression. Common hurdles such as fear of confrontation, the tendency to over-explain, or the inclination to shrink back can often keep you from saying what truly needs to be said. These hurdles are not insurmountable, though they may feel daunting and persistent.

The fear of confrontation is a significant obstacle. The mere thought of potential conflict can trigger a cascade of anxiety, leading you to freeze or avoid the conversation altogether. This fear often stems from past experiences where voicing your needs resulted in negative outcomes or misunderstandings. To steady yourself:

- Practice grounding techniques before the conversation, such as slow, steady breathing to calm racing thoughts.

- Focus on the calm, centered presence you wish to bring rather than potential worst-case outcomes.

- Process lingering emotions in a quiet moment afterward instead of letting them spiral.

Overexplaining is another common barrier to clear communication. It often arises from a desire to justify your needs or to prove to others that you're being "reasonable". This can dilute your message and create confusion, leading to misunderstandings at best. At worst, it becomes a trap: by providing a reason, you inadvertently invite others to "solve" your problem or negotiate your boundary. To avoid this, aim for brevity. State your expectations in simple terms, and resist the urge to elaborate. For example, if declining an invitation, "I can't attend this time" is sufficient. There is no need to share your alternative plans; doing so only invites debate. This approach values both your needs and the listener's capacity to understand and accept your limit without unnecessary complexity.

The habit of shrinking back often stems from a deeply ingrained survival mechanism: the belief that staying small keeps the peace or ensures your safety. This reflex is frequently born from past environments where taking up space or voicing a preference invited conflict, rejection, judgement or volatility. In those contexts, "disappearing" was a skill used for self-preservation. However, in your adult life and professional career, this once-useful shield can become a cage. When you shrink, you are essentially editing yourself out of your own experience to avoid the perceived risk of being seen. Building the confidence to stand tall is an incremental process of proving to your nervous system that it is now safe to be heard:

- **Begin with low-stakes boundaries.** Practice saying "no" to a casual favor or expressing a minor preference in a safe environment.

- **Log your successes.** Let each successful interaction serve as evidence that the world does not collapse when you speak your truth.

- **Trust the momentum.** Over time, your comfort will grow as the behavior becomes a habit rather than a hurdle.

As you navigate this resistance, remember that change is a result of repetition and consistency. Realize that every conversation is a step toward decisive self-expression. The goal is not a flawless performance, but steady progress; each attempt strengthens your ability to articulate your position with conviction.

Overcoming these patterns is a trajectory of growth and continuous learning. Be deliberate as you adopt new ways of interacting with the world. Each effort you make contributes to a sharper understanding of yourself and the relationships you choose to cultivate. As your comfort grows through practice, so will your capacity for authentic conversation that honors both your own needs and the needs of those around you.

Assertiveness is an evolving skill set that requires persistence. The more you engage with it, the more intuitive it becomes, eventually transforming once-dreaded encounters into opportunities for genuine connection. Allow this process to unfold at its own pace, trusting your ability to adapt as you reclaim your voice.

Refining Boundaries Over Time

Life presents itself as a dynamic flow, with changes that ripple through your daily experiences and alter the landscape of your needs, desires, and interactions. Limits aren't static lines drawn in sand. They are more like rivers, needing regular attention, care, and occasional redirection to serve their purpose effectively. Periodically assess whether a boundary still serves its intended function. This ongoing process ensures that your standards evolve as you do, adapting to new circumstances and growth.

Practical tools for managing your personal space often start with *journaling* and *self-reflection*. Writing about your experiences helps you notice patterns and evaluate whether your current limits truly protect your energy or if you're still ending up depleted and overcommitted. Over time, this awareness sharpens the language of your boundaries, making them clearer and more in tune with who you are and what you value today. Beyond tracking where adjustments might help, journaling also leaves you with a tangible record of your growth. It's a quiet reminder of how far you've come.

Periodic self-check-ins offer another powerful way to keep your needs aligned with your life's changes. Choose a rhythm that feels realistic. It can be weekly, monthly, or quarterly. In these moments of pause, gently explore:

- Are the lines I've drawn still working as I intended?

- Do any feel too rigid or too loose for my current situation?

- Have new situations emerged that call for clearer limits?

Look at different areas (personal, professional, social, and emotional), and consider whether tweaks might bring better balance. These observations aren't just about spotting problems, but they're also about honoring your progress. Celebrate moments when you upheld your need, navigated a hard conversation, or simply said "no" without overexplaining. Recognizing these wins, no matter how small, builds trust in your ability to stay true to yourself while remaining open to change.

In doing this work, remember: boundary-setting isn't static. It's an ongoing practice and an act of self-care that evolves as your life, values, and relationships do.

The refinement process is about continuous improvement rather than striving for perfection. It allows for flexibility, letting your choices and limits breathe and grow along with you. Changing boundaries is not a sign of failure' it is an indication of growth and development. Life's unpredictability means that what works today might not work tomorrow, and that's perfectly okay. The key is to remain open to change and willing to reassess your needs regularly, adapting as new challenges and opportunities present themselves.

Aim for a balance between being firm and being flexible. This ensures that while you protect your core needs, you also remain open to life's ebb and flow. This adaptability fosters resilience, allowing you to respond effectively to new opportunities without compromising your well-being.

Adjusting your personal limits is vital for maintaining healthy relationships with yourself and others. It is an ongoing practice that requires care but ultimately leads to deeper satisfaction. Setting clear lines is not just about defense; it is about creating a life where you can thrive, where your values are honored, and where your aspirations find their place.

As we close this chapter, recognize that this practice is a powerful part of a larger journey. The next step is learning to integrate these limits into your daily life with emotional intelligence. In the next chapter, we will explore how self-awareness and empathy become the bridge between intention and action, helping you navigate complex dynamics while staying true to your values. Through this lens, boundaries evolve from static rules into living practices that enrich both your relationships and your sense of self.

CHAPTER 9

STEP 3: EMOTIONAL INTELLIGENCE

Designing a boundary is only part of the work. The real test often comes in the moments when that boundary is challenged, questioned, or misunderstood. In those situations, your ability to stay grounded emotionally determines whether the boundary holds or quietly erodes. Emotional intelligence provides the steadiness needed to respond with clarity rather than react from guilt, fear, or frustration.

Strengthening Emotional Resilience

Emotional resilience is the internal anchor that keeps you steady when your boundaries are tested. At its heart is self-awareness: the ability to notice the thoughts, feelings, and physical signals that indicate you are approaching a limit. Practicing mindfulness, such as focusing on your breath or scanning your body for tension, helps you recognize these early cues before stress escalates into a reactive state.

Journaling deepens this awareness. Recalling on moments when your limits were crossed and noticing how you responded can reveal where your lines might need strengthening. Furthermore, this practice builds emotional intelligence by helping you comprehend the "why" behind your reactions. A journal acts as a tool for self-discovery, promoting a deeper understanding of your own needs and steering you toward more intentional interactions.

Building self-trust is the foundation of every boundary-related decision. If past experiences have caused you to hesitate, start with incremental steps: pause when you feel depleted, or decline a task that feels overwhelming. Each choice that honors your needs adds a layer of confidence. Looking back on the moments when you held your ground serves as a necessary reminder of your progress. When you trust yourself to protect your own well-being, you can engage with others more deeply without the fear of losing your balance.

This internal security is what allows you to use empathy effectively without compromising your position. Empathy is a powerful tool for connection, but it can leave you drained if you overextend. Balancing empathy with assertiveness protects your emotional energy. This requires staying aware of your own needs while still caring for others. Notice the moment your giving shifts from genuine compassion to reflexive people-pleasing. Setting clear limits does not close you off; rather, it ensures your interactions remain healthy and sustainable.

With consistent practice, these tools help you respond thoughtfully rather than reacting out of fear or guilt. Over time, resilience becomes a quality you carry into every conversation, not just a temporary measure you reach for in difficult moments.

Review and Recalibrate: When Empathy Overreaches

To maintain your balance, analyze recent interactions where empathy may have resulted in overextension:

- **Identify a specific instance** where excessive empathy compromised your limits.

- **Evaluate the alternative:** Consider how balancing that empathy with self-care would have altered the outcome.

- **Plan your future approach:** Determine a strategy to maintain this equilibrium in similar interactions moving forward.

This exercise offers a clear view of your patterns, allowing you to course-correct with grace. By weaving emotional intelligence into your boundary-setting, you create space for healthier bonds and a more grounded sense of self. Each reflection builds your capacity to move through life with greater understanding and command.

Emotional Regulation in Boundary Conversations

Emotional regulation transforms boundary conversations from intimidating encounters into manageable interactions. Preparing mentally and emotionally before entering discussions where your comfort zones may be tested is profoundly effective. Begin by setting a clear intention: commit to remaining composed and articulate, regardless of any internal discomfort.

Grounding techniques anchor you both before and during these discussions. Consider the following methods to maintain your center:

- **Box Breathing:** Inhale for four counts, hold for four, exhale for four, and pause for four. This rhythmic cycle calms racing thoughts and centers your focus.

- **The 5-4-3-2-1 Sensory Scan:** Silently note five things you see, four you can touch, three you hear, two you smell, and one you taste. This process pulls your awareness into the present moment and eases rising anxiety.

- **Nature Grounding:** If possible, tune into natural sensations such as the breeze on your skin or the feel of the ground under your feet. These subtle cues steady your breath and slow a reactive mind.

These practices ensure you communicate from a place of clarity rather than reacting from tension or fear. As you find your internal center, let that stability extend to your physical presence. Utilizing centering body language, such as relaxing your shoulders, maintaining soft eye contact, and speaking in slow, deliberate tones, reinforces your verbal message. These physical cues do more than project confidence to others: they signal to your own nervous system that you are grounded and safe. Techniques like focusing on your breath or holding a grounding object like a smooth stone keep you present, preventing emotional overwhelm.

From this steady vantage point, you can adopt the perspective of a detached observer. Viewing the interaction through a lens of neutral curiosity allows you to use non-reactive language and hold your ground without escalating tension. This stance creates the necessary space for productive dialogue while safeguarding your emotional energy. Assuming the role of a detached observer can be empowering. It allows you to use non-reactive language, holding your grounds without escalating tension. This approach creates space for productive dialogue while safeguarding your emotional energy.

Post-interaction, it's important to engage in stress-reduction strategies to avoid emotional exhaustion. Decompression rituals, such as journaling about the experience or engaging in physical movements like stretching or walking, to help process residual tension. You might also try "body shaking," a natural reset used by animals in the wild to discharge stress after a tense encounter. While it may feel silly at first, shaking your limbs in the privacy of your home or even a bathroom stall can literally move the physical charge of stress out of your body. Seeking support from others who value your boundary-setting efforts is another useful resource to unwind and reset. It provides reassurance and encouragement.

Self-compassion is essential during this phase. Acknowledge that you're doing hard, necessary work and deserve credit for each step toward healthier, more authentic interactions. Acknowledging your efforts with affirmations like, "I accomplished something challenging, and I'm proud of myself." This type of personal validation bolsters your resilience and creates a positive feedback loop that encourages ongoing growth.

To reset emotionally before re-engaging with the person or situation, consider allocating time for activities that soothe and replenish you. Whether indulging in a favorite hobby or taking restful breaks, these moments allow emotions to settle. This pause is a deliberate step in maintaining equilibrium rather than an act of avoidance. It ensures that when you revisit the conversation or environment, you're equipped with a fresh perspective and renewed strength, ready to re-engage constructively.

Strengthen Conflict Navigation Skills

Navigating conflict with composure transforms tense interactions into opportunities for mutual understanding. When met with defensive or resistant responses, maintain a neutral, steady tone: this defuses tension, signals calm authority, and keeps the conversation anchored in respect. While emotions may flare, phrases such as "I hear your concerns, but my decision remains unchanged," can de-escalate a situation swiftly. This approach validates the other person's feelings while firmly upholding your position.

Should a conversation veer toward hostility or become unproductive, be ready with a pre-planned exit strategy. Stating, "Let's pause and revisit this later," provides the necessary space to regroup and approach the issue with fresh insight.

Replacing defensiveness with curiosity shifts the dynamic from confrontation to collaboration. Instead of impulsively reacting, try inquiring, "What makes that difficult for you?" This question invites the other person to share their perspective without feeling attacked, and it also fosters an environment geared toward joint problem-solving. If a conversation becomes emotionally unsafe, exiting gracefully can be a wise choice. Have a plan for such scenarios, allowing both parties time to reflect and reassess before re-engaging in the discussion.

Effective problem-solving relies on this ability to remain anchored in your values even while seeking a resolution. Assertiveness is not an obstacle to collaboration; it is the framework that makes it possible. Redirecting conversations when someone persistently crosses a line can be challenging, but it is necessary to keep the dialogue productive. Scripts like, "I acknowledge your perspective, but I need this limit for my well-being," affirm your needs without dismissing theirs. This equilibrium ensures you remain true to yourself while acknowledging the other person. Collaboration is not about compromising your core values: it is about identifying common ground and understanding an alternative viewpoint without sacrificing your own.

Recognizing when a discussion has devolved into a power struggle is crucial for preserving your emotional energy. Conversations that spiral into debates over who is "right" seldom lead to productive outcomes. If you notice tension rising, you might attempt co-regulation by inviting the other person to pause with you. Try a direct approach: "This is an important conversation and I want to stay present for it. Can we both take a few deep breaths before we continue?"

Taking this moment to breathe together can settle the nervous systems of both parties, creating a more stable foundation for dialogue. This invitation acts as a final attempt at connection. However, if the other person is unable or unwilling to meet you in that calm space, prioritize a pause over a forced resolution. If co-regulation fails, or if the interaction remains a battle of wills, utilize your exit strategy. Remember: upholding your personal guidelines does not necessitate the other person's agreement or validation. Your boundaries exist to safeguard your well-being, not to placate others or gain approval.

In these moments, trust your intuition to decide when to continue and when to withdraw. Prioritizing emotional safety over immediate resolution prevents unnecessary strain and preserves your energy for more constructive engagement later. By staying anchored in your values, you ensure that every interaction, even the difficult ones, fosters a healthier dialogue with yourself.

Recovery from Setbacks

When you establish a limit only to see it buckle under self-doubt or external pushback, the experience can be discouraging. These moments are an inevitable part of the process. Internally, you may question the validity of your needs or fear that you are being unfair; externally, others may test your resolve through subtle pressure or open resistance. Life itself often presents unpredictable challenges that force you to rethink and readjust your position.

Rather than viewing these moments as failures, treat them as essential opportunities for refinement. Use these instances to evaluate your approach: determine if your current strategy still fits your needs or if a new adjustment would serve you better. Sometimes standing firm is the answer, while at other times, a shift in tactics provides the breakthrough you need. This level of awareness is what ultimately solidifies your resolve.

To maintain momentum through setbacks, focus on these core practices:

- **Incremental Progress:** Practice asserting yourself in low-pressure situations to build your confidence "muscle."

- **Regular Reflection:** After an interaction, objectively note what felt aligned and where you felt a sense of friction.

- **Strategic Support:** Surround yourself with individuals who respect your space and encourage your development.

- **Intentional Acknowledgment:** Mark small victories, such as expressing a need clearly or holding your ground even when it felt uncomfortable.

Change is rarely linear. It is an ongoing process shaped by patience, repetition, and self-compassion. Over time, you will recognize that setbacks do not erase your progress: they shape it. They reveal what truly matters to you and provide the clarity needed to step forward with greater self-awareness.

Persistance and flexibility are what keep you moving when the path feels unsteady. With every experience, you are refining the skill of living with authenticity and self-respect. You are actively crafting a life where your needs have a rightful place. Recognize that setbacks do not define your journey; they mold your character. They are not roadblocks, but rather stepping stones toward deeper empowerment.

As we close this chapter, reframe every challenge as a source of valuable insight into your growth trajectory. Let these experiences inform your path, fostering more balanced relationships and a life of greater integrity.

The journey continues with Step 4: Boundary Mastery. In the next chapter, we will explore how to sustain these changes over time. We will look at ways to keep your ground strong and adaptable as your life evolves, ensuring your boundaries continue to nurture personal growth, resilience, and lasting connection.

CHAPTER 10

STEP 4: BOUNDARY MASTERY

Boundaries do more than protect your time and energy. They shape the way you live. When your limits are maintained consistently, your daily choices begin to reflect your values, beliefs, and priorities. Boundary mastery is the process of sustaining that alignment over time, allowing you to live an authentic and intentional life.

Maintaining Boundaries Over Time

We have already established that boundaries are not rigid walls; rather, they are the steady markers that guide your daily life. Now that you have learned to identify and set these markers, the focus shifts to Mastery. True mastery occurs when your boundaries move from being conscious choices to becoming reflexive habits.

Think of consistency as the act of putting on a uniform each morning. Just as a professional uniform signals your role and responsibilities without the need for daily debate or decision-making, your boundaries eventually become a seamless part of how you engage with the world. When your values and beliefs serve as this core "uniform," you no longer have to negotiate with yourself in the heat of the moment: you are simply operating within your established identity. This consistency creates clarity for others and protects your internal energy.

Daily rituals reinforce this stability. Consider integrating the following practices into your routine:

- **Morning Affirmation:** Start each day with a clear intention, such as: *Today, I honor my needs and value my limits.*

- **Mindfulness Practice:** Spend a few quiet moments focusing on your breath to tune in to your emotional state.

- **Evening Reflection:** Ask yourself if you communicated your needs clearly and protected your energy. Journaling these answers tracks your progress over time.

When you wear a uniform, you don't just look the part; you are equipped with the specific tools required for the job. In the realm of boundary mastery, anchor phrases serve as these essential tactical tools. They provide a steadying influence in moments of uncertainty, allowing you to respond with clarity rather than reacting from a place of stress. By having these phrases ready, you remove the need for "on-the-spot" negotiation, ensuring your responses remain aligned with your core values even when you are under pressure. Preparation turns discomfort into intention, allowing you to communicate with steadiness.

Consider these tailored options for various scenarios:

- **For General Capacity:** *I am currently at my limit for new commitments, so I will have to decline this invitation* *to ensure I can give my best to my existing responsibilities.*

- **For Emotional Capacity:** *I want to be fully present for this conversation, but I do not have the bandwidth to give it the attention it deserves today.*

- **For Personal Space:** *I value our connection, but I need some solitary time this evening to recharge.*

- **For Unannounced Visits:** *I appreciate you stopping by, but I am not in a position to host guests right now. Let us schedule a time in advance for our next visit.*

- **For Intrusive Questions:** *I am not comfortable discussing that topic, but I am happy to talk about [alternative topic] instead.*

- **For Financial Requests:** *I have a personal policy of not lending money to maintain the health of my relationships. I am happy to support you by helping you brainstorm a plan.*

- **For Chronic Crisis/Rescuing:** *I can see you are in a difficult spot, but I am unable to step in as a financial safety net. I can, however, help you look for community resources that specialize in this area.*

- **For Digital "Always-On" Culture:** *I have moved to checking my messages at specific times during the day to stay focused. I will get back to you during my next window.*

- **For Scope Creep at Work:** *I would be happy to help with this new task; however, we will need to decide which of my current priorities should be moved to the back burner to make room for it.*

- **For the "Guilt Trip" or Peer Pressure:** *I hear how much* *this matters to you, but I have to stick to my original 'no' to ensure I don't overextend myself. I hope you can understand.*

- **For Direct Resistance:** *I understand that this is difficult, but my decision is based on what I need to stay effective.*

Over time, these phrases will move from being "scripts" to being a natural extension of your voice. You will find ways to adjust the words, cadence and delivery so they feel true to you. These tactical tools handle your daily interactions, long-term mastery requires a regular maintenance schedule. Your needs are not static, and the boundaries that served you last month may require adjustment as your circumstances evolve. To stay steady, consider setting monthly goals that focus on one area to strengthen at a time. If overcommitting is a recurring issue, you might practice declining one nonessential request each week. Sharing these goals with a trusted friend or support group can add a layer of encouragement and accountability.

Honoring your limits is not about rigidity; it is about being attentive and adaptive. Life changes, and so will your boundaries. What matters is your commitment to revisit and refine them, ensuring they still support your well-being and match your values. These small, steady practices build the resilience and confidence needed to sustain standards that feel both authentic and flexible. Each effort, no matter how minor, contributes to a life where your needs are acknowledged and respected by others and by yourself.

Holding the Line: Your Weekly Boundary Log

To transform boundary-setting from a reactive act into an intentional habit, take a moment at the end of each week to document your progress in a dedicated log. Use these three prompts to keep your awareness sharp:

- **The Win:** What line did I uphold successfully this week?

- **The Friction:** Where did I struggle to maintain my ground, and what allowed that to happen?

- **The Adjustment:** What is one specific "tool" or anchor phrase I will use next week to improve?

By incorporating this practice into your routine, you create a foundation for long-term success. While this process requires patience and a willingness to adapt, this consistent effort ensures your needs are honored. This dedication paves the way for more fulfilling relationships and a balanced life.

Resilience and Recovery after Boundary Violations

Boundary violations are an inevitable aspect of social and professional life. These breaches typically stem from two sources: unintentional misunderstandings or intentional overstepping. Misunderstandings often arise when communication is vague, leaving room for assumptions. Conversely, intentional breaches may be driven by another person's desire for control or manipulative tendencies. Distinguishing between these two dynamics is critical for your recovery. While miscommunications can often be resolved with patient clarification, intentional overstepping requires a more robust and decisive response to preserve your peace and integrity.

When a boundary is breached, your nervous system typically shifts into a reactive state, which can cloud your judgment and lead to defensive posturing. To counter this, you must develop the skill of strategic detachment. This practice allows you to create a "psychological buffer" between the violation and your response. Rather than absorbing the impact, you observe the event as if you were a neutral third party. This perspective shifts your focus from the personal sting of the event to an objective analysis of the interaction.

To cultivate this detachment, utilize the Neutral Observer technique during moments of friction. Mentally step back and narrate the situation in the third person: *"I am observing an attempt to bypass a stated limit regarding my schedule."* This simple shift in language prevents the internalization of blame and keeps you anchored in your identity.

Complement this mental pivot with Peripheral Vision Grounding. When you feel the "tunnel vision" of stress or anger, deliberately soften your gaze and expand your awareness to include the space to your far left and far right without moving your eyes. This works because foveal vision, the sharp, central focus used to look at a screen or a person's face, is linked to your sympathetic nervous system, or your "fight-or-flight" response. By switching to peripheral vision, you manually stimulate the parasympathetic nervous system, which signals to your brain that the immediate threat has passed. This physiological override lowers your heart rate and restores your ability to think clearly.

The Post-Breach Strategy: **Reassert, Revise, or Release**

By integrating physiological grounding into your daily routine, you ensure that when a breach occurs, you are restoring balance from a position of strength and maintaining control of your trajectory. Once you have regained this clarity, you can move into an effective recovery plan. This involves taking specific steps to regain control and reinforce your personal space against future intrusions.

Begin with a reflection exercise to identify the specific trigger of the violation. Ask yourself: *What allowed this line to be crossed? Was it a lack of clear signals, an assumption of leniency, or a blatant dis-*

regard for my stated limits? Once you have pinpointed the cause, you must decide on the most effective strategic action:

- **Reassert:** This involves a firm conversation to reinforce established expectations. Speak clearly about how the violation impacted you and define the specific changes required to move forward.

- **Revise:** At times, a boundary requires adjustment to better fit your current needs and circumstances. This is not a sign of failure; it is an act of intelligence that might involve setting more explicit terms or narrowing your accessibility to the individual involved.

- **Release:** In cases where a person or situation continually disregards your needs, the most resilient choice is to step back. Letting go might mean distancing yourself from a specific project or a relationship that no longer supports your well-being.

Seeking support from trusted friends or mentors during these transitions can provide the valuable outside perspective needed to aid in your decision-making.

Recovering from boundary violations requires both patience and persistence. It involves accepting that your requirements for safety and respect will naturally evolve as you grow. By treating every breach as a lesson rather than a failure, you build a resilient framework that supports your long-term health. This ongoing process empowers you to navigate your relationships with confidence, knowing that your boundaries are not rigid walls, but flexible and firm anchors for your life.

Building a Resilient Mindset

Cultivating resilience in the face of criticism is the final pillar of boundary mastery. Whether the pressure originates from external sources or your own internal dialogue, your response dictates your long-term stability. Self-critical thoughts often masquerade as motivation, yet they serve only to drain the cognitive energy required to maintain your standards. To master your mindset, you must replace self-judgment with Strategic Curiosity. Instead of fixating on the perceived failure of a boundary, analyze the interaction as a data point. Ask yourself what specific variable changed in the interaction that you can account for next time. This shift transforms a setback into a necessary step for your personal evolution.

To sustain this perspective, you must curate a High-Utility Feedback Loop. Surround yourself with individuals who offer objective insights rather than emotional noise. Establish regular check-ins with these mentors or peers to ensure you are receiving a steady flow of calibration, which transforms criticism from a source of anxiety into a professional tool for refinement. This solution-oriented approach further transforms internal barriers into architectural puzzles. When you encounter a situation where asserting yourself feels difficult, do not view it as a personal deficit. Instead, treat it as a design challenge. Identify the specific friction point and brainstorm actionable steps to mitigate it.

This proactive mindset fuels growth by encouraging you to operate at the edge of your comfort zone. As you refine these problem-solving skills through role-playing or incremental goal-setting, your confidence in handling high-stakes situations will grow. You are no longer merely defending yourself; you are executing a well-rehearsed protocol. This resilience is the anchor that maintains your position during periods of high pressure. True mastery requires a balance between staying grounded in your values and remaining open to necessary adaptation. This prevents your boundaries from becoming brittle or resistant to the natural changes in your professional and personal environment.

Continuous integration of new lessons is the final component of this framework. Seek out opportunities for skill enhancement through workshops, literature, or reflective practices that offer insights into your developmental progress. By setting aside dedicated time to review your experiences, you foster a mindset that welcomes evolution without losing sight of your core identity. Mastery is not defined by a single leap, but by these steady, intentional steps. By facing criticism with curiosity, sharpening your problem-solving architecture, and remaining a student of your own experiences, you provide yourself with a sturdy footing for any challenge.

Valuing Others While Advocating for Yourself

Navigating the delicate balance between self-advocacy and care for others begins with the precision of your language. This involves utilizing Subjective Clarity to articulate your needs without casting blame. Instead of focusing on the perceived failures of others, articulate your internal state with specificity. This ensures that your message is clear yet non-confrontational, maintaining mutual respect even during a disagreement. To refine these skills, seek out advanced workshops or courses that focus on the architecture of healthy self-expression and professional negotiation. I personally found immense value in a six-week assertive communication course offered by my healthcare facility. This provided a controlled, safe space to test the boundaries of my current comfort level alongside others who were navigating similar challenges.

An unintentional but vital benefit of this group setting was the "mirror effect" it provided. By interacting with individuals who were just beginning their journey, I gained a clear benchmark of my own progress. It is often difficult to see how far you have evolved until you observe your previous habits reflected in someone else. This experience reinforced that mastery is a continuous cycle of testing, adjusting, and reflecting.

Practicing active listening is equally critical in this phase of mastery. By genuinely tuning into the perspectives of others, you acknowledge their experience, which builds the rapport necessary for sustainable boundaries. In emotionally charged situations, utilize your prepared scripts as a guide to navigate the conversation with poise. Developing the skill to draw lines with empathy involves more than just selecting the right words; it requires a mindset that honors both personal integrity and relational harmony. Crafting empathic boundary-setting conversations allows you to express care without sacrificing your own requirements.

Techniques for negotiating mutual boundaries are essential for long-term relational health. These strategies involve identifying common ground where both parties feel respected and heard. This might require adjusting plans or recalibrating expectations to find a middle path where both your needs and those of others are acknowledged. When negotiations become challenging, consider seeking mediation from a neutral third party. This professional oversight can facilitate communication and uncover hidden solutions that satisfy the core values of everyone involved.

You must build trust through consistency and transparency. When your actions align with your words, you establish a reputation for reliability. This consistency assures others that your boundaries are not arbitrary or reactive; rather, they are thoughtfully considered aspects of your self-care strategy. Over time, this transparency nurtures stronger bonds and a shared sense of awareness. Reflective practices play a significant role in assessing and improving the balance between empathy and assertiveness. Use journaling prompts to explore your communication style and identify if you tend to prioritize others at your own expense.

Engaging in open dialogues with mentors or peers allows you to refine your approach by learning from both successes and setbacks. Collaborating with a coach or therapist can further enhance your growth, helping you cultivate a communication style that values both your boundaries and those of others. In summary, advocating for yourself while respecting others is a dynamic process involving compassionate communication, empathy, and constant reflection. By developing these skills, you strengthen your position while enhancing the quality of your connections. This balance is not static; it evolves as you grow.

Every conversation is an opportunity to practice these advanced skills. In the next chapter, we will bring these ideas into your professional life, exploring how these guidelines become practical tools for empowerment at work. By turning these principles into daily actions, you will learn to navigate workplace dynamics with confidence, shaping a career path that honors both your well-being and your highest ambitions.

Pause for a Moment

"Using your voice is an act of agency. Sharing your experience helps others discover their own."

Lorilee Lucas

If what you have read so far helps you see your life with greater clarity, I would be most grateful if you could **consider leaving a brief review.**

Your review helps this work reach others who may be quietly searching for the clarity and confidence you are building.

If you feel moved to share your experience, you can scan the QR code below to leave a brief review or a star rating.

With appreciation,

PART 6

WHERE IT BECOMES REAL

CHAPTER 11

BOUNDARIES IN ACTION:

PROFESSIONAL EMPOWERMENT

Boundaries become meaningful when they are applied in the places where expectations, relationships, and pressure intersect. It is one thing to understand your limits in theory, and another to hold them steady in environments where responsibilities, personalities, and competing priorities are constantly in motion.

The workplace is often where these skills are tested most consistently. Deadlines, team dynamics, and shifting priorities can quietly blur the line between commitment and overextension. Learning to communicate clear professional boundaries protects not only your time and energy, but also your credibility, effectiveness, and long-term career growth.

Assertiveness in Professional Environments

Step into a bustling office, where conversations blend with the quiet rhythm of keyboards. This daily scene is the landscape where your professional boundaries take shape. In this environment, boundaries do more than protect your time; they serve as a catalyst for your career. When you master the art of the professional boundary, you demonstrate a level of self-governance that leadership prizes. This clarity often leads to accelerated promotions, merit-based raises, and a deep sense of trust with executives who see you as a leader who can manage both high-stakes projects and personal bandwidth with equal precision.

Standing in your authority becomes a bridge between silence and overreaction, equipping you to navigate professional waters with clarity. This means standing firm for your own requirements while honoring those of others. When achieved, this delicate balance fosters workplace harmony and creates an environment where every contributor can thrive. In this setting, expressing yourself openly shifts how colleagues perceive you, significantly enhancing your credibility and reliability. Communicating with poise demonstrates that you are both thoughtful and decisive, which showcases your leadership potential and deft handling of interpersonal relations.

Finding your voice in discussions requires persistence and a readiness to evolve your approach. One helpful technique is to frame your language around your professional requirements. For instance, rather than saying, "You never give me enough time," try, "I need more time to complete this task effectively." This shift keeps the focus on your operational experience and avoids placing blame, which fosters a more constructive dialogue. Equally important are your nonverbal cues. Confident posture, relaxed shoulders, and steady eye contact reinforce your message, often speaking louder than words. These subtle signals convey self-assurance and set the tone for balanced conversations.

Conflicts are inevitable, but handling them proactively ensures they become opportunities for growth rather than roadblocks. Professional models like the Interest-Based Relational Approach emphasize understanding underlying issues and seeking win-win solutions. When disputes arise, respond with composure. For instance, if a colleague interrupts you, an assertive response might be, "I value your input, but I would like to finish my point first." This honors both perspectives while holding your ground and encouraging mutual understanding.

Challenges in self-advocacy often arise from a fear of retaliation or negative judgment. However, speaking up is not about confrontation; it is about honesty and consideration. Building self-assurance through professional development can be transformative, offering tools designed for real-life application. In these supportive spaces, you can grow comfortable sharing your voice, gently shifting from self-doubt to conviction while learning to handle challenges with ease.

Try It Yourself: Craft Your Confident Response

Think back to a recent work situation where being more assertive might have changed the outcome. Use the following prompts to recalibrate your approach:

- **Analyze the Barrier:** What stopped you from speaking up? Was it a concern regarding perception or a lack of prepared language?

- **Audit the Impact:** How did the silence affect your productivity or emotional energy afterward?

- **Draft the Pivot:** Sketch out how you could approach

the situation differently. Draft talking points that center your needs, remain respectful of team goals, and maintain steady body language.

Practice this revised approach in a low-pressure setting, such as with a trusted mentor or a peer. Ask for honest feedback, noticing how your tone feels when spoken aloud. This is not just a rehearsal; it is a vital step toward strengthening your professional presence. Over time, these small, mindful practices transform how you navigate meetings and negotiations. Each attempt builds a sturdier foundation for authentic communication at work and beyond.

Navigating Team Dynamics with Confidence

Once you have strengthened your individual presence, you must apply those same principles to the collective ecosystem of your team. Understanding team dynamics involves more than just interpersonal harmony; it requires Strategic Alignment. Each contributor represents a distinct role that must integrate seamlessly to serve organizational goals. Clear roles and responsibilities provide the structural integrity that prevents overlap and confusion. When every member comprehends their specific remit, friction decreases and productivity enhances. This clarity is especially vital in cross-functional teams, where varied perspectives must be managed with precision to spark innovation rather than misunderstanding.

Communication serves as the operational engine of collaboration. Active listening and constructive feedback foster an environment where high-value ideas flow freely. True active listening involves grasping the underlying intentions behind a colleague's words, while constructive feedback offers the objective insights necessary for professional growth. Together, these practices create a culture grounded in trust. This openness ensures that every team member feels empowered to contribute their unique strengths, effectively transforming diversity into a competitive advantage.

Defining clear structures within your team protects individual focus and ensures workflows remain consistent. These frameworks include guidelines for professional discussion and explicit expectations regarding availability. Clarifying response windows helps manage the team's mental load, ensuring members know when they can expect assistance and when they are permitted to disconnect. By establishing these operational boundaries, teams work more efficiently without encroaching on personal space, fostering an environment that prioritizes long-term well-being alongside immediate productivity.

Power dynamics also influence how team boundaries are established and respected. While hierarchical structures often dictate authority, it is essential to empower all team members to express their operational needs. Navigating these challenges involves recognizing the influence of power on interactions and advocating for equitable treatment. Strategies such as Upward Feedback Mechanisms allow team members to voice concerns or suggest improvements without fear of retribution. Empowering individuals at every level fosters a culture of shared responsibility, creating a more balanced and resilient team dynamic.

Reflect and Refine: Your Team Boundary Blueprint

Analyze how your team functions on a daily basis. Identify where your personal requirements and the team's workflow align, and where they create friction. Use the following steps to calibrate your environment:

- **Identify the Friction Point:** Isolate one specific area where a clearer boundary could ease tension or boost collaboration.

- **Implement Tactical Steps:** Brainstorm concrete actions to address the issue, such as setting aside blocks for deep focus, scheduling consistent weekly syncs, or defining explicit response windows for digital messages.

Documenting these steps makes the commitment tangible, while regular reviews keep the strategy relevant. Building healthier team dynamics is not merely about guarding your time; it is about nurturing transparent communication and honoring each person's contribution. With commitment, intentional boundaries shift from being perceived as walls to becoming pathways built on trust and shared success. They become part of the team's everyday rhythm, ensuring that collaboration remains genuine, sustainable, and productive.

Communicating Needs to Superiors and Peers

Individual presence is the foundation, but strategic communication is the tool that builds your career. When approaching superiors or peers, utilize Value-Based Framing to highlight mutual benefits. For instance, explain how additional resources enhance team productivity and achieve shared goals. Use concrete data to support your requests, anchoring your needs in facts that resonate with organizational objectives. This approach demonstrates a commitment to collective success, making it easier for others to support your perspective. When your needs resonate with organizational goals, your boundary transforms from a personal request into a strategic recommendation. Leadership prizes this level of alignment.

Negotiating capacity with supervisors is an essential skill for maintaining operational integrity. Initiate these conversations with professional poise. When discussing workload, you might perform a Capacity Audit and to articulate your limits while acknowledging the organization's priorities. For example, when a workload becomes unsustainable, you might say: *"I understand the importance of this project. To ensure its success and maintain our quality standards, I need to clarify my current capacity and prioritize my existing deliverables."* Transparency paves the way for effective negotiation. It fosters a cooperative atmosphere where both your limits and the team's requirements are respected, effectively forcing a collaborative prioritization.

Clear lines with your peers further enhance collaboration. When you establish consistent communication, you create a foundation of trust. Clarifying roles and limits for collaborative projects early ensures that everyone understands their responsibilities. For instance, set expectations around deadlines and availability to prevent misunderstandings. This level of transparency strengthens professional relationships and contributes to an efficient workflow where each member feels understood. When every contributor knows the "rules of engagement," the team moves faster and with greater precision. Clarity is not a luxury; it is a requirement for high-performance teamwork.

Communicating these boundaries will inevitably present challenges. Expect resistance. You may encounter skepticism when you first express your needs, but your professionalism remains your best defense. Maintain your composure. Reiterate your requirements with steady conviction. If a situation becomes high-stakes, leverage an accountability partner or mentor to provide an objective perspective. By staying true to your professional standards, you reinforce the legitimacy of your boundaries.

In summary, effectively communicating your needs involves stating requests clearly and negotiating with care. Build relationships through radical openness. This approach creates a workplace where personal space is respected and growth feels systematic. Every interaction is an opportunity to refine your presence. Move your career forward with integrity and unshakeable confidence.

Managing Time and Energy to Prevent Burnout

Strategic communication protects your professional reputation; energy management protects your life. When your daily schedule is consistently packed with competing tasks, it is easy to miss the subtle indicators of exhaustion. Listen to your body. Persistent fatigue, muscle tension, or a growing irritability are rarely passing phases. They are often quiet signals. Physically and emotionally, burnout can manifest as a creeping sense of dread regarding your workload. Recognizing these indicators early allows you to intervene before the stress becomes systemic. Setting thoughtful boundaries serves as a gentle defense against this decline. By establishing clear limits on your commitments, you ensure your focus remains sustainable.

Managing your time effectively makes a significant difference in avoiding depletion. Complexity often masks itself as urgency. To counter this, consider utilizing the Eisenhower Box to separate what is truly important from what is merely loud. This tool helps by categorizing every task into one of four quadrants. Quadrant one contains tasks that are both urgent and important. These are the "fires" that require your immediate attention, such as a looming project deadline or a crisis. While you cannot ignore these, the goal is to manage them efficiently so they do not consume your entire day. Quadrant two holds tasks that are important but not urgent, such as strategic planning, skill development, and relationship building. Mastery involves intentionally carving out time for this quadrant; it is the proactive work that eventually reduces the number of fires in quadrant one. Quadrant three involves tasks that are urgent but not important, like unnecessary meetings or certain types of administrative email. While you may not be able to delegate your entire inbox, you can delegate specific tasks or use automation to minimize the time spent here. Finally, quadrant four consists of time-wasting activities that are neither urgent nor important, which you should aim to eliminate to protect your bandwidth. Focus your energy on tasks that align with your long-term priorities. Allow yourself to delegate or delay the rest. When you use this framework, your day begins to feel purposeful rather than reactive.

By using this framework, you can channel your energy toward tasks that align with your long-term priorities. Time-blocking methods also enhance productivity by dedicating specific hours to particular tasks. Rather than constantly switching between your inbox and deep work, you assign set windows for administrative duties and separate, protected windows for high-value projects. This minimizes "context switching," allowing you to regain control over your schedule and reduce overwhelm in a proactive manner.

Establishing personal lines for work-life balance creates a buffer between your professional responsibilities and personal life. Start by defining clear work hours, allowing yourself time to unwind without the intrusion of work-related concerns. Disconnecting requires a ritual. You might set your devices to "do not disturb" at a specific time each evening. Creating a physical transition, such as a walk or a dedicated reading period, signals to your brain that the workday has concluded. These practices signal to your brain that it is time to relax, which is essential in preserving your overall well-being. This separation remains essential for preserving your long-term well-being. Self-care is not a luxury; it is a vital requirement for sustaining your energy.

Allow yourself regular breaks. A sharp mind thrives on moments of stillness. Integrate activities that bring you genuine joy, whether through creative outlets or quiet reflection. These moments provide a necessary respite from high-pressure environments. Mindfulness practices, such as deep-breathing exercises or meditation, offer powerful ways to de-escalate workplace tension. By centering yourself in the present moment, you alleviate anxiety and cultivate the resilience needed to maintain your enthusiasm.

Boundaries are the anchors that steady you. They allow you to engage fully with your work while preserving the essence of who you are outside of it. As we conclude this chapter, remember that your career is a marathon. In the next chapter, we will look at how these same principles shape your personal life. We will explore how thoughtful boundaries help you navigate social situations and manage the anxiety that can arise in your private world. You will see that these standards support emotional balance in every corner of your life.

CHAPTER 12

BOUNDARIES IN ACTION:

SOCIAL INTERACTIONS AND ANXIETY

Social situations can be some of the most complex places to hold your boundaries. Unlike the workplace, where roles and expectations are more clearly defined, social environments often carry unspoken rules about politeness, belonging, and approval. When anxiety enters the picture, it becomes even harder to trust your instincts or speak up for what you need.

Strategies for Overcoming Social Anxiety

Social anxiety rarely waits for you to arrive at a crowded room. It often begins at home, manifesting as a heavy hesitation while you get ready or a recurring urge to cancel your plans at the last minute. By the time you find yourself at a lively party, where the air is thick with laughter and overlapping conversations, your nervous system may already be on high alert. Your heart might race as if you have run a sprint, your palms may turn clammy, and a quiet desire to slip away unnoticed starts to take hold. In these moments, anxiety acts like an intruder, bringing waves of uncertainty that threaten to overshadow your presence and prevent you from engaging with the people around you.

Understanding the specific triggers and patterns that spark this response is the first step toward regaining your composure. For many, the apprehension of meeting new people, the pressure of public speaking, or the sheer scale of a crowded event serve as frequent instigators. To identify your personal patterns, introspection is essential. Look back at past social situations where discomfort began to creep in and notice if repetitive themes emerge. This reflective practice allows you to turn a vague sense of dread into a clear map of your triggers. By recognizing these initiators of discomfort, you gain the insight needed to prepare for them proactively. This self-awareness transforms your experience from a passive struggle into a journey toward social assurance.

Upon identifying these sources, the focus shifts to managing the physical sensations of anxiety before they become overwhelming. Because the most intense tension often occurs during the transition into a social space, establishing a pre-event ritual is a powerful way to settle your mind. Nadi Shodhana, or alternate nostril breathing, is a sophisticated tool for this purpose. It is best practiced in private, such as in your car or a quiet room, to balance your nervous system before you engage with others. To practice this, find a comfortable seat. Use your right thumb to close your right nostril and inhale deeply through the left. At the peak of your breath, close the left nostril with your ring finger, release the thumb, and exhale through the right. Inhale through the right side, then switch to exhale through the left. This cycle communicates a message of safety to your body, allowing your physical tension to dissolve.

Once you enter a social setting, your focus shifts to maintaining that internal balance without drawing unwanted attention. This is where you begin to implement Stealth Boundaries, which are internal actions that protect your energy while you are in the presence of others. If you feel the familiar surge of adrenaline while standing in a group, you need tools that are virtually invisible to an observer.

Coherent Breathing is an excellent in-the-moment rescue. This involves breathing in through your nose for a count of five and out through your nose for a count of five. There is no holding of the breath and no obvious physical movement. It is a subtle, invisible way to regulate your heart rate variability while you are actively engaged in a conversation. Another practical, hidden tool is Progressive Muscle Relaxation. You can systematically tense and release muscle groups that are hidden from view, such as your toes, calves, or thighs. This practice offers physical relief from the "bracing" reflex that anxiety triggers, where the body physically prepares for a threat that isn't there. These techniques act as anchors, providing a sense of control over your physiological responses without alerting those around you.

These physical tools serve a larger purpose: they provide the stability required to enforce your Social Boundaries. When your anxiety is high, it is difficult to say "no" to an intrusive question or to end a draining conversation. By using Coherent Breathing to lower your heart rate, you regain the presence of mind to honor your limits. For example, rather than feeling forced to stay in a conversation that has become overwhelming, a regulated nervous system allows you to calmly state, "It has been great catching up, but I'm going to step away for a moment to get some air." In this way, managing your anxiety becomes the foundation for maintaining your integrity in any social interaction.

To build long-term resilience, you might consider the practice of Gradual Exposure. This involves expanding your comfort zone through small, incremental steps. Start where you feel capable. If large events feel overwhelming, you might begin by attending a small gathering for a short duration with a pre-planned exit time. This exit time is, in itself, a boundary you set with yourself to ensure you do not become overextended. Each successful interaction serves as a building block for your confidence. You could initiate a brief conversation with a familiar acquaintance or join a group centered around a specific hobby where the activity takes the pressure off the conversation. Relish each step forward. Regardless of the size of the gesture, it represents a victory over the patterns of the past.

Mindfulness remains a steady ally when your thoughts begin to spiral. It helps you return your focus to the present moment rather than getting swept away by "what if" scenarios. You can use grounding techniques like the 5-4-3-2-1 method, which can be done entirely in your head. Identify five things you see, four you can touch—like the fabric of your sleeve or a cold glass—three you hear, two you smell, and one you can taste. This is a cognitive boundary that prevents your mind from wandering into self-criticism. These small daily practices shift your focus from internal worry to external presence. Over time, you may find that you are interacting more genuinely with those around you, allowing your social connections to feel authentic and sustainable.

Mirror Practice: Speaking Your Boundaries

Find a quiet space where you can stand in front of a mirror without distractions. Take a few moments to center yourself. Before you begin speaking, use the Coherent Breathing technique we explored: inhale for five seconds and exhale for five seconds. Notice how your body feels when it is regulated. This is your "baseline of power," and your goal is to speak from this steady state rather than from a place of tension.

Choose Your Script: Select a specific boundary you want to practice. It could be something simple like, "I'm not comfortable sharing that," or a practical exit line like, "I've enjoyed this conversation, but I'm going to go circulate now."

Observe the Non-Verbals: As you speak the words out loud, look at your reflection. Notice if your shoulders hunch or if your voice drifts into a higher, more uncertain pitch. Practice keeping your posture open and your chin level. Real authority is often found in the stillness of your body rather than the volume of your voice.

Experiment with Tone: Repeat the phrase three times using different inflections. The first time, say it as a question; notice how it feels like you are asking for permission. The second time, say it with aggression; notice the unnecessary tension in your jaw. The third time, speak it as a neutral fact—like you are telling someone the time of day. This neutral tone is the "Mastery" standard for professional and social boundaries.

Identify the Resistance: Notice where you feel physical pushback in your body. Does your chest tighten? Do you find it hard to maintain eye contact with yourself? Acknowledge these sensations without judgment. They are simply old patterns of social anxiety meeting your new commitment to self-respect.

Returning to this exercise helps you become familiar with the sound of your own authority. It strengthens your confidence and makes real-life practice feel more natural and grounded. Through this gentle recognition, you are not forcing change overnight. You are learning your own rhythm. Each honest observation and quiet act of courage becomes another thread in the tapestry of self-trust, guiding you toward calmer, more genuine social moments.

Authentic Self-Expression in Social Situations

Once you have practiced the sound of your own voice in the mirror, the next step is ensuring that voice represents your true internal state. Authentic self-expression is the practice of maintaining congruence, which is the alignment between your internal values and your external behavior. When you operate with this level of clarity, your actions and words naturally gain strength. This is not about oversharing or performing. It is about moving away from the "roles" you feel forced to play and toward a way of being that remains consistent across different environments. This genuine approach becomes the foundation for trust-filled relationships because people feel the stability of your character.

To express yourself genuinely, you must first identify the "mask" you might be wearing to feel safe. A helpful tool for this is the Johari Window, a framework used to categorize what parts of yourself you share with the world and what parts you keep hidden due to fear of judgment. Mastery involves slowly expanding your "Open Area," which is the quadrant containing information known to both you and others, by sharing small, honest truths. This does not require a confession. It simply means admitting a quirk, sharing a sincere opinion, or speaking about a passion that you usually downplay to blend in. By identifying which values anchor your life, you can ensure your social behavior remains consistent with who you are when you are alone.

When interacting with others, maintain your integrity through transparent communication. Utilize "I" Statements to transform potential conflicts into constructive dialogue. This is a primary tool for assertive authenticity. Rather than saying, "You always change plans at the last minute," which triggers defensiveness, try, "I feel overwhelmed when schedules shift abruptly because I value predictability." This shift is subtle but powerful. It centers the conversation on your internal experience, which is an indisputable fact, rather than the other person's behavior, which is an accusation. Sharing personal insights in this way shows vulnerability without losing your authority.

While authenticity offers significant rewards, real barriers like the fear of rejection can cast a shadow over your progress. These fears often stem from societal expectations that urge you to conform rather than stand out. To navigate these barriers, focus strictly on what you can control: your own thoughts and your commitment to your values. Everyone perceives the world through their own unique experiences. This means their judgment of you is actually a reflection of their own history, not your inherent worth. Counteract the pressure to blend in by curating a Supportive Inner Circle of individuals who value your sincerity. When you are surrounded by people who respect your boundaries, your confidence to be yourself grows exponentially.

By choosing to show up as your genuine self, you build relationships that feel real because they are based on truth rather than a performance. Each conversation becomes an opportunity to test your alignment. Dedicate time to Congruence Checks throughout the day. Ask yourself, "Does this response reflect my true opinion, or am I just trying to keep the peace?" Authenticity is not a destination you reach. It is a series of small, intentional choices you make in every interaction. As you practice those choices, social anxiety begins to lose its grip because you no longer have a "character" to maintain.

Building Confidence in Social Interactions

True social confidence is not about a flawless performance; it is built on a foundation of Self-Trust. Social anxiety often stems from an internal fear that you will not protect your own boundaries when they are challenged. If you do not trust yourself to say "no," to leave early, or to disagree with a popular opinion, every social event feels like a threat to your autonomy. As you master your internal boundaries, your social anxiety naturally decreases. When you know with certainty that you will honor your own limits, you no longer need to fear the influence or judgments of others. You are no longer entering a room to "survive" the people there; you are entering it as a person who is fully in charge of their own experience.

To nurture this confidence, you can develop a routine that reinforces your competence through specific, repeatable actions that build this internal contract.

Micro-Visualizations: Before entering a social space, spend a moment visualizing yourself successfully holding a boundary. Focus on the physical details: the steadiness of your breath when you decline an invitation or the calm clarity of your voice when you change a topic. By pre-playing these moments of self-advocacy, you prove to your nervous system that you are a reliable protector of your own peace.

Competence-Based Affirmations: Rather than using vague positive thinking, use statements that focus on your capacity to remain aligned. Try, "I trust myself to honor my energy levels," or "I have the tools to exit a draining conversation." These reminders focus on your internal agency rather than seeking external approval, which provides a more stable foundation for your confidence.

Strategic Practice: Seek out low-stakes environments to test your new internal boundaries. This might include community classes, volunteering, or hobby groups. These spaces allow you to practice being assertive without the high pressure of established social circles. Each time you honor your preference, you add a building block of evidence to your self-trust.

Social setbacks are inevitable. They are not failures of your character but data points for your growth. Moments of awkwardness offer opportunities for introspection. Develop a protocol for Resilience in Response to Setbacks. When an interaction does not go as planned, acknowledge the emotion without harsh self-criticism. Ask yourself, "What specific part of my internal boundary was challenged, and how can I recalibrate for next time?" This analytical approach keeps you in a growth mindset, ensuring that a single stumble does not derail your progress.

Empathic Listening and Assertive Replies

Confidence is the internal foundation, but the way you communicate that confidence determines the quality of your external connections. When you have established a baseline of self-trust, you gain the capacity for Non-Defensive Presence. This is the ability to listen deeply to others without feeling that their words or emotions are a threat to your own boundaries. Empathic listening then becomes a high-level skill rather than a social burden. It allows you to understand the emotions and intentions beneath a person's words, giving you the clarity needed to set boundaries that are effective and respectful.

To master this, utilize the OARS model: Open-ended questions, Affirmations, Reflections, and Summaries. This framework ensures you are focused intently on the speaker without prematurely planning your own response. Reflective listening, where you echo back the essence of what you heard, provides the other person with the reassurance that their thoughts are understood. For example, saying, "It sounds like you are feeling pressured by the current deadline," shows that you have processed their reality. This technique lowers the temperature of the room, making it much easier for you to introduce your own needs next.

Finding the balance between listening deeply and standing firm in what you need is the hallmark of a mature communicator. By honoring both empathy and assertiveness, you create space for conversations rooted in mutual understanding. When expressing your truth, use the "Yes, And" method of communication to bridge the gap. You might say, "I see your point about the urgency, and I need to stick to my original schedule to ensure the quality of the work." These simple lines allow you to speak your truth calmly and firmly, keeping the dialogue balanced without losing sight of your own limits. This approach promotes awareness of both perspectives and opens the floor for constructive exchanges rather than a battle of wills.

Even the most mindful communicator can find certain moments unexpectedly intense. When discussions heat up, give yourself permission to utilize a Tactical Pause. Shift your attention to something steady, like the sensation of your feet on the floor or the texture of the chair beneath you. This simple gesture helps you stay present without feeling swept away by the other person's energy. In navigating complex conversations, remember that maintaining empathy does not equate to conceding your boundaries. It means recognizing all emotions without letting them dominate the outcome. If you encounter resistance, articulate your intentions calmly and pose questions that encourage exploration over confrontation.

Mastering the blend of empathic listening and assertive replies enriches every relationship you have. Each dialogue becomes an opportunity to connect thoroughly and express yourself genuinely. As you cultivate these skills, you will notice a significant increase in your confidence. These tools are not limited to single moments; they ripple outward, shaping the tone and depth of your life as a whole.

In the next chapter, we will turn our attention inward. We will explore how setting and honoring internal boundaries becomes a vital part of healing, self-respect, and reclaiming the parts of yourself that may have been overlooked or surrendered along the way.

CHAPTER 13

BOUNDARIES IN ACTION:

HEALING AND PERSONAL RECLAMATION

Boundaries do more than solve individual situations. Over time, they begin to change the way your life feels. Each time you honor your limits, trust in yourself grows. That growing self-trust makes it easier to speak clearly, choose relationships that respect you, and step away from situations that do not. The process begins to reinforce itself. What once felt difficult gradually becomes natural. Boundaries stop feeling like something you have to enforce and start becoming the way you move through the world.

Rebuilding Self-Esteem Through Boundaries

The previous chapter gave you the tools to survive a crowded room. This chapter is about the person who enters that room. You might have mastered the art of small talk or learned how to steady your breath, but true peace comes from knowing you will not lose yourself the moment someone else starts talking. We often become strangers to ourselves by perpetually quieting our own instincts to accommodate the demands of others, eventually losing the ability to distinguish our own voice from the expectations of the world. Authentic expression is only possible when you are no longer a stranger to yourself.

When you establish internal boundaries, your social anxiety naturally begins to settle because the threat of being overwhelmed by others is mitigated by your own commitment to self-advocacy. You are no longer looking for the exit in the room because you carry that exit within your own ability to say no. This internal sovereignty is the cornerstone of self-worth. Healing is the process of closing the gap between who you had to become or were told to be, and who you actually are.

Whether you are recovering from a toxic relationship or a period of high social anxiety, guarding your personal space is more than a survival tactic; it is the active reclamation of your autonomy. These standards are the structural framework of your new life. They are the visible evidence of your worth, affirming your right to exist without constant interference. Every time you set a boundary, you make a tangible commitment to yourself, reinforcing personal values that may have been suppressed for years. By consistently honoring these limits, you transform the abstract concept of self-care into the concrete foundation upon which you rebuild your self-esteem.

To cultivate a resilient self-image, you must replace negative external scripts with objective internal truths. Mastery involves using Evidence-Based Affirmations that focus on your capacity and rights. Phrases such as "I have the right to decline requests that drain me" or "My perspective is a valid data point" are harder for the inner critic to dismiss. You can strengthen this by performing a Belief Audit. Write down a lingering doubt, such as "I am difficult for wanting space," and counter it with a factual correction: "I am a person with limited energy who requires recovery time." Over time, this practice aligns your inner dialogue with the respect you deserve.

Begin by introducing modest boundaries into your daily life. This might look like reserving ten minutes each morning for undisturbed solitude or choosing not to answer non-urgent texts after a certain hour. Treat every instance where you honor these limits as a data point for your growing self-trust. Each of these moments reinforces your confidence and reminds you of your power to safeguard your peace. As these practices become habitual, they foster a deeper awareness of what you truly need, moving you from a state of constant reaction to a state of intentional action.

Overcoming self-doubt in boundary-related decisions requires strategies that reinforce your newfound confidence. When you feel the urge to retract a boundary, engage in Cognitive Restructuring to challenge the validity of the doubts undermining your resolve. When faced with hesitation, ask yourself whether these doubts are rooted in reality or fear-based assumptions. Journaling can be a powerful tool here, offering a space for self-reflection and growth. Write about instances where you've successfully maintained your ground and explore how those experiences felt. By documenting specific instances where you successfully maintained your ground, you create a Success Log. This log acts as objective evidence of your progress, serving as a resource you can revisit whenever doubt creeps in to remind yourself of your actual capacity for resilience.

Beyond internal reflection, seeking inspiration from role models who embody a strong sense of self can be highly beneficial. Observe individuals who move through life with a balance of grace and assertiveness. Identify the specific qualities you admire in them, such as how they phrase a refusal, how they maintain eye contact, or how they handle interruptions without apologizing for their space. These observations provide a practical blueprint for your development, reinforcing the fact that healthy boundaries do not alienate others; they earn respect.

Body Boundary Visualization: Feeling Your Limits

Internalizing these boundaries often requires a physical connection to your sense of space. Find a quiet area where you can sit or stand comfortably. Close your eyes and take several slow, grounding breaths.

- **Proprioceptive Awareness:** Bring your attention to the air immediately surrounding your body. This is your personal sphere.

- **Mental Delineation:** As you breathe, "trace" this boundary with your mind, noticing it around your arms, torso, and the space just in front of your face. Visualize this not as a rigid wall, but as a flexible, protective perimeter that belongs solely to you.

- **Strengthening the Perimeter:** Bring to mind a situation where your boundaries have felt unclear. As you visualize the scenario, consciously reinforce the protective space around yourself. Feel the steadiness in your posture as you maintain this limit.

- **Body Cues:** Notice any sensations in your body. Look for tightness, relaxation, warmth, or lightness. These physical signals are your early warning system. Learning to recognize them allows you to set a boundary the moment your body feels crowded rather than waiting for an emotional outburst.

Practicing this visualization consistently helps you connect with your body's natural cues, reinforcing your limits and building confidence in honoring your needs. This intentional pause is not about achieving perfection. It is about tracing the quiet progress that builds resilience, ensuring your boundaries become reliable guides toward a life lived true to who you are.

Healing from Narcissistic Relationships

The internal safety you cultivate through visualization is often the first thing targeted in a high-control or narcissistic relationship. In these dynamics, boundaries are not just ignored; they are systematically dismantled through manipulation. This erosion of your "inner sanctuary" is why survivors often carry emotional scars that run deep. These dynamics, marked by manipulation and control, can leave you questioning your own reality and worth. Recognizing the impact of this manipulation is the first step in healing. Emotional scars often manifest as chronic self-doubt, hyper-vigilance, or a lingering sense of inadequacy. It is essential to understand that these feelings are not a reflection of your value; they are remnants of a toxic environment. Acknowledging these symptoms without judgment allows you to view them as catalysts for change rather than permanent damage, beginning the process of making peace with your history.

Emotional detachment from a narcissist is an act of reclaiming personal power. To begin this transition, you must practice mental compartmentalization. Imagine an "Inner Sanctuary" similar to your physical boundary visualization: a mental space untouched by their words or presence, where your thoughts and feelings belong solely to you. You can return to this center whenever you feel the old scripts of manipulation start to rise. Mindfulness practices, such as focusing on a steady breath or a simple mantra like "I am free to choose," create the mental distance necessary to reinforce your autonomy. These techniques are not about forgetting the past, but about releasing its hold on your present. By integrating these habits into your routine, you cultivate a mindset of ongoing liberation.

Rediscovering your identity after such a relationship is like piecing together a puzzle that was intentionally scattered. Identity Reconstruction involves intentionally looking for the pieces of yourself that existed before the manipulation began. Start by asking fundamental questions: What interests genuinely resonate with you? What values do you hold when no one is watching? Engage in activities that once brought you joy, independent of past influences. Setting small, personal goals helps reorient you toward your true self. These goals should reflect who you are now, not who you were told to be. Every step you take toward these personal milestones is a step away from the shadow of past manipulation.

Support is invaluable in this journey. Online support groups and forums can offer a sense of community and validation from those who have walked similar paths. These spaces provide proof that your experience was significant and that recovery is possible. Recommended reading on narcissistic abuse can also offer strategic insights for moving forward. Books and therapeutic practices tailored to survivors provide guidance on navigating complex emotions and rebuilding confidence. Consider exploring creative outlets like art, music, or writing as forms of self-exploration. These pursuits can rekindle your passion for life and act as a medium for emotional release, guiding you toward a vibrant identity that was always yours to begin with.

Your path to healing is deeply personal, yet you are not alone in this process. The journey from surviving to thriving involves reclaiming your voice, understanding your worth, and setting boundaries that protect your newfound clarity. In doing so, you cultivate resilience and rediscover the vibrant identity that was always yours to begin with. The path of healing is one that strengthens with each step forward.

Transforming Fear-Based Communication

Reclaiming your identity is an internal victory, but your voice is the primary tool you use to maintain that territory in the real world. For many, fear-based communication has been a lifelong survival tactic, developed to avoid conflict or criticism by silencing your own needs. Over time, this becomes a barrier to sincere expression. To dismantle this habit, you must first identify your specific fear triggers. These might surface as a racing heart before speaking up or a reflexive urge to agree when you actually want to dissent. Understanding these responses as echoes of past trauma is liberating. They are not your fault, nor are they insurmountable. By acknowledging their origins, you empower yourself to slowly dismantle their hold and move toward a more authentic way of relating.

Moving beyond fear-driven habits calls for practical, hands-on strategies and requires patience rather than pressure. Consider exploring boundary-setting in settings that feel safe and manageable. This could involve softly declining a casual invitation, sharing a small preference in a comfortable conversation, or voicing a minor need in a familiar environment. If it feels supportive, role-playing with a trusted friend can provide a low-stakes space to find words that feel right for you. Some find that workshops or classes focused on self-expression offer a helpful structure, providing a community of others who are also learning to navigate these waters. These often include guided exercises rooted in everyday scenarios, offering both structure and feedback. Over time, these practices help replace hesitation with clarity and conviction, turning assertiveness into a familiar, natural part of your interactions.

Building a secure style of expression is a journey of small, meaningful steps. You might choose to focus on subtle ways to build your self-assurance, such as maintaining comfortable eye contact or allowing yourself the time to speak slowly and clearly. As you move at your own pace, you may find that confidence begins to follow your actions. This growing assurance helps you share your thoughts with more freedom, eventually allowing your voice to emerge from the shadow of fear. With time and self-compassion, these new rhythms can mature into a steady, natural way of connecting with others.

Personal growth is a lifelong evolution of how we interact with the world around us. You may find it grounding to hold a few long-term intentions for your communication, such as being more present with loved ones or feeling more grounded in your professional life. Breaking these intentions into small, manageable moments allows you to notice and celebrate every bit of progress. If you feel ready, seeking gentle feedback from mentors or friends you trust can offer new perspectives on your growth. This process is not about reaching a final destination of perfection, but about honoring the progress you have made and the person you are becoming.

As you feel your confidence expand, you might find yourself drawn to new opportunities for expression, such as participating in group discussions or exploring public speaking. These experiences can offer fresh perspectives on your adaptability and further enrich your ability to connect with others. Each new interaction is an opportunity to discover another facet of your voice.

Unsent Letters: Finding Your Voice

Set aside a quiet moment where you will not be interrupted. This exercise is an invitation to speak your truth freely, in a space where your words are for you alone. It is a safe laboratory for exploring your voice without the pressure of an audience.

1. **Choose Your Audience:** You might write to someone who crossed a boundary or perhaps to a younger version of yourself who was doing their best to stay safe.

2. **Allow the Words to Flow:** Write openly about your feelings, your needs, and your perspective. Give yourself permission to express exactly what you feel without the need to edit or censor.

3. **Observe with Kindness:** As you write, notice any emotions that surface. If you feel hesitation, guilt, or shame, simply acknowledge those feelings as part of the process.

4. **Reflect on the Discovery:** Take a moment to consider what your words reveal about your needs and the strength of your voice.

Write about what you discover and revisit your notes over time. Notice patterns, celebrate progress, and refine your approach as you grow. Returning to this exercise helps you uncover hidden fears, clarify your needs, and practice giving your voice space, building courage and confidence in speaking up for your needs.

Establishing Safe and Supportive Connections

In the realm of healing, the people you surround yourself with can either uplift you or pull you down. Building safe and supportive networks is crucial for ongoing growth and recovery. These relationships are characterized by understanding and a shared commitment to each other's well-being. They offer a sanctuary where you can express yourself freely without fear of judgment. Within such a community, you find encouragement to explore your true self and the assurance that you are not alone in your struggles. This sense of belonging can be a powerful catalyst for personal transformation.

To identify healthy relationships, it's important to look for certain key traits. Supportive individuals cherish your boundaries and celebrate your achievements without envy or competition. They listen without interrupting, offer constructive feedback, and are present when you need them. In contrast, red flags in potentially harmful relationships include manipulation, constant criticism, or an imbalance where one person gives significantly more than they receive. Learn to trust your instincts. If someone's presence consistently leaves you feeling drained or anxious, it might be time to reevaluate that bond. Your intuition is a guiding light in recognizing what relationships serve you.

Developing new habits in your relationships can feel like a big shift, but it is how you protect the progress you have made. You can start by simply speaking your needs out loud early on. For example, you might tell a new acquaintance: "I'm focusing on a more balanced schedule right now, so I'm keeping my weeknights for personal time. I'd love to connect on Saturday, though." Using clear statements like this takes the guesswork out of personal space. In any social setting, you have the right to be honest about what you need and to say no without feeling the need to over-explain. A healthy connection will respect those limits. You can test the waters with small requests and simply notice whether the other person honors your space or tries to push past it.

Beyond individual friendships, finding a community that aligns with your healing allows you to practice your autonomy on a larger scale. This is not just about social engagement; it is about Conscious Integration. Whether through support groups, shared-interest clubs, or volunteer work, these spaces act as a training ground for your new boundaries. In these environments, you can observe how a healthy group dynamic operates. This is a space where shared experiences create bonds without requiring you to sacrifice your individuality. Engaging actively in these circles does not just expand your network: it reinforces your sense of purpose, proving that you can belong to a group while remaining entirely true to yourself.

To visualize this growth, you might consider creating a personal support map that outlines your closest contacts and highlights areas where you might seek new relationships. This map serves as a visual reminder of your network's strength and potential areas for development. By mapping out who provides emotional support, who offers practical help, and who shares your interests, you gain a clearer picture of your social landscape. An evolving support map reflects your journey, illustrating both stability and the healthy growth of your relationships as you move forward.

Keep in mind as this chapter concludes that relationships, like gardens, require nurturing to thrive. Safe and supportive connections not only bolster your healing process but also pave the way for a life enriched by genuine interactions and mutual growth. By deepening these connections and strengthening your voice, you will find yourself meeting life's twists and turns with greater steadiness and grace. In the next chapter, we will explore the expansive possibilities that emerge when boundaries become more than protective lines. They become pathways toward growth, freedom, and deeper fulfillment. Through this lens, your reclaimed self does not just endure; it begins to truly flourish.

PART 7

WHAT BECOMES POSSIBLE

CHAPTER 14

What Freedom Feels Like

Freedom has a lightness to it. The day unfolds with a quiet sense of ownership over your time, your energy, and your choices. Conversations feel simpler because you are no longer carrying the responsibility of managing everyone else's expectations. Decisions come with a steady confidence that your needs matter just as much as anyone else's. In the pages that follow, you will see how this freedom begins to show up in everyday life: in the way you manage your energy, navigate relationships, express your identity, and move through the world with a calm sense of self-possession.

From Burnout to Balance: A Life of Sustainable Energy

There is a specific kind of exhaustion that comes from living without limits. It often begins the moment the day starts, feeling less like a fresh beginning and more like a negotiation with a mounting debt of obligations. When boundaries are absent, mornings are often spent scanning a list of demands that belong to everyone else. True freedom arrives when that chronic weight is replaced by the realization that personal energy is a finite, high-value asset, and decisions are guided by a commitment to peace rather than pressure. This is the practical result of the foundations established in previous chapters. It is a shift from a life of frantic damage control to a life of intentional pacing. With firm boundaries in place, the need to live in a defensive crouch disappears, allowing the day to be met on one's own terms.

This transformation turns personal boundaries into the functional infrastructure of vitality. They serve as a buffer against the cultural pressure to overextend, ensuring that a "yes" is a strategic choice rather than a reflexive response to external pressure. When you stop sacrificing your well-being to rescue others, you reclaim the hours and mental bandwidth necessary to pursue the work and interests that actually move the needle in your life. There is a difficult but liberating truth at the center of this mastery: human worth is not a currency earned by enduring unnecessary pain.

As these practices take root, emotional clarity naturally sharpens. It becomes easier to recognize the physiological warning signs of overwhelm before a total breakdown occurs. In this stage of growth, rest is no longer viewed as a guilty indulgence or an emergency measure; it is a calculated part of a long-term performance strategy. This creates a new baseline where being centered is the norm and high stress is the anomaly.

This approach to energy management is what makes a life sustainable. By orchestrating a deliberate rhythm between high-output action and restorative pause, the system begins to replenish itself. The goal is no longer just to survive the week, but to maintain a way of living that feels as natural and steady as breathing.

Mapping Your Boundaries in Action

Set aside a quiet moment. Let your thoughts wander through the shape of your usual day, from morning to night. Notice the points where your energy dips, where your patience wears thin, or where guilt starts whispering.

Now jot down three choices you could make this week to guard your energy:

- Perhaps it's turning down a meeting that doesn't serve your priorities.

- Maybe it's stepping away from your desk for a real lunch instead of eating at the screen.

- Or simply protecting an hour in the evening that belongs only to you.

As you list these choices, consider the objective gain: how will honoring these limits improve your mental clarity and physical stamina? This exercise is about more than just saying no. It is about actively designing the architecture of your day so that your time remains a reflection of your own priorities: balanced, deliberate, and sustainable.

From People-Pleasing to Personal Power

Personal power begins when your needs transition from quiet thoughts to spoken truths. This is the end of the internal trial where you constantly cross-examine your own desires to see if they are "allowable" by others. In this stage of mastery, your worth is not a theory you hope others will validate: it is a fact you affirm through your actions. Boundaries serve as the mechanism that makes this possible, freeing you from the compulsion to suppress your own identity for the sake of a false harmony. You no longer show up only when it serves someone else's agenda; you occupy your life fully and without apology.

As the habit of seeking external approval fades, you discover the vital distinction between fitting in and true belonging. Fitting in is a hollow negotiation; it requires you to scan a room and change who you are to be accepted. It is an act of betrayal against the self. True belonging, however, only occurs when you have the courage to present your authentic self, regardless of the reaction. This requires a shift in perspective: you realize that you do not need to find a place to belong because you already belong to yourself. By anchoring in your own values, you stop trying to buy entry into social circles through self-sacrifice. This internal groundedness allows you to relate to others from a position of genuine sincerity rather than a desperate need for a seat at the table. The ultimate realization is that you belong anywhere you decide to show up.

Self-trust becomes your primary tool for navigation. When your instincts signal that a line must be drawn, you honor that signal without a second round of self-doubt. You have stopped outsourcing your decisions to the people who benefit most from your compliance. You are now your own center of gravity, rooted in self-assurance. Instead of doubting your intuition, you rely on it, knowing it steers you toward a life where you are seen and valued on your own terms. In this space, personal power is a lived reality that transforms every interaction you have with the world.

From Chaos to Clarity: Emotional Peace Through Boundaries

A life without boundaries is inherently noisy. It is filled with the constant mental rehearsal of past conversations and the preemptive defense of future ones. True emotional peace arrives when you move through the day with a steady mind, unburdened by this internal chatter. Boundaries provide the mental stillness necessary to transform overthinking into tranquil clarity. When you belong to yourself, you no longer need to litigate every social exchange in your head to ensure you were accepted. Instead, a peaceful mind becomes a refuge: a place of reliable inner calm that offers solace regardless of external circumstances.

This clarity is fueled by a commitment to nervous system regulation. When peace and calm become your North Star, you begin to evaluate every interaction through the lens of your own biological safety. You no longer ignore the tightening in your chest or the shallowing of your breath. Instead, you use these physical signals as a compass, adjusting your boundaries in real time to maintain a state of regulation. You are no longer willing to trade your physiological peace for someone else's comfort.

Emotional resilience grows as you learn to weather life's storms by staying rooted in your identity rather than slipping into the role of a victim. In this stage of growth, you no longer seek validation through commiseration or the retelling of the unfairness of it all. You recognize that replaying the trauma in search of someone else to save you only keeps you tethered to the past. By maintaining clear lines, you stay grounded in the core of your own life, moving through turbulence without being swept away by the narrative of the injury. You are the observer of the storm, not a character trapped in its story.

As you stand firm in your own truth, your interactions become cleaner and more direct. You gain the ability to discern what truly belongs to you and what belongs to someone else. This allows you to effortlessly deflect guilt, projection, and manipulation. The power these tactics once held over you diminishes because there is no longer a hook for them to catch on. You are no longer reacting to the static of other people's emotional baggage; you are responding from a place of grounded, intentional peace.

From Reactive to Intentional Relationships

The hallmark of relationship mastery is the transition from a defensive posture to an intentional presence. This shift is grounded in more than psychology; it is rooted in the literal physics of human connection. Studies suggest that the heart produces a powerful electromagnetic field extending several feet beyond the body. When two people enter each other's proximity, their nervous systems begin a process of electromagnetic entrainment, where heart rate variability and physiological rhythms attempt to synchronize.

Understanding this biological reality changes the "why" behind your boundaries. If you are constantly engaging with dysregulated individuals, your system works overtime to maintain its rhythm. Freedom is the ability to break this cycle of reflexive entrainment. By being intentional about whose energy you allow into your immediate space, you are practicing a high-level form of biological stewardship. You are no longer a passive receiver of other people's emotional static: you are the primary governor of your own energetic state.

As you apply these energetic filters, you stop being a magnet for those who seek to stabilize their own chaos using your regulated energy. Misaligned relationships begin to fade naturally, without the dramatic exits or turmoil that once defined your past. Boundaries clarify who genuinely belongs in your inner circle, allowing you to channel energy toward connections that encourage mutual growth. When you are grounded in your identity, you become a higher-value connection to others because your presence is steady rather than reactive.

In this space of safety, honesty becomes your primary language of love. Vulnerability is shared freely as a gift rather than demanded as a proof of loyalty. This creates a foundation for trust that does not hinge on constant reassurances. You no longer feel confined by the expectations of others; instead, you experience a sense of liberation within your connections. You engage genuinely, fostering relationships where both parties prosper together. By belonging to yourself first, you ensure that those who remain in your life share your values and your vision for a supportive, balanced future.

From Workplace Stress to Professional Empowerment

Professional empowerment is the transition from a state of constant availability to a state of strategic contribution. In a culture that often rewards the loudest or the most accessible, a profound act of mastery is defining the terms of engagement. Workplace stress is frequently the result of an "open door" policy that has shifted into a revolving door for other people's priorities. With the establishment of firm professional boundaries, the role shifts from being a reactive resource to a high-value asset. This provides the agency to decide which tasks merit brilliance and which are merely peripheral.

This shift is rooted in the protection of deep-work capacity. By setting clear limits on communication and availability, the cognitive space necessary for high-level problem solving is preserved. The goal is to ensure that every output is of the highest possible quality. There is a movement away from the frantic "busyness" of answering every notification toward the intentional pacing of a professional who knows the value of time. Boundaries in the workplace serve as a filter, ensuring that energy is directed toward the goals that generate the greatest impact for a career or an organization.

As these standards are implemented, professional identity begins to evolve. The reputation of being the person who always "squeezes it in" is replaced by that of someone who respects their own workflow. This mastery of a schedule naturally earns the respect of colleagues and leaders alike. When limits are honored, it signals to the world that time is a premium commodity. This clarity eliminates the resentment that often builds from feeling exploited, replacing it with a sense of calm authority. Work is no longer done to satisfy the shifting expectations of the office: it is done to fulfill an internal standard of excellence.

Empowerment also extends to the handling of professional conflict and negotiation. With a grounded sense of self-belonging, it becomes easier to advocate for needs, such as a deadline extension, a resource request, or a pay increase, without the interference of people-pleasing guilt. Requests become negotiable rather than mandatory, and self-assurance invites understanding rather than conflict. In this space, professional power is not something to wait for a promotion to receive: it is a lived reality brought to the table every single day.

Finally, work-life harmony becomes a tangible goal when personal time is treated as a non-negotiable asset. Disconnecting from work pressure occurs without the need for excessive explanations, creating a balance that nurtures both spheres. This harmony allows for a full immersion in responsibilities and passions alike. These guidelines ensure that effort leads to fulfillment rather than fatigue, crafting a life where contributions are celebrated and well-being is a prioritized constant.

From Lost Identity to Honest Self-Expression

Boundaries serve as the essential framework for identity recovery. For many, the ability to identify personal opinions, beliefs, and desires was subverted at a young age: often a necessary tool for survival within environments where staying "small" was the only way to remain safe. Mastery in this stage involves a deliberate turn inward to rediscover the voice that was muted by the expectations of others. It is the process of reclaiming the internal data: preferences, passions, and purpose that have long been treated as secondary to the needs of the room. This recovery reminds the self that who you are truly matters.

This process is a restoration of the core self. When boundaries are established, they create a protected space where personal values are no longer distant echoes but the primary guides for daily choices. Instead of scanning the environment for cues on how to behave, the focus shifts to an internal compass. This allows for a version of self-expression that is no longer diluted by the weight of external approval. This alignment between internal truth and external action, expressed through attire, words, and choices, signals that the period of conforming to societal molds is over. The transition is marked by a move from reactive compliance to an intentional, sovereign presence.

As this internal authority solidifies, self-approval replaces the constant urge to please others, providing a sense of profound liberation. Decisions are made in alignment with this rediscovered essence, creating a life where one is not just surviving, but truly thriving. Creativity and honesty flourish because the fear of judgment no longer holds the power to self-censor. The ability to explore new ideas and express emotions freely is backed by the validation and celebration of a unique creative voice. Life is no longer a performance staged for the benefit of others: it is a vibrant manifestation of a life lived true to its own design, without restriction or compromise.

From Fear-Based Living to Empowered Expansion

Personal standards foster the environments necessary for aspirations to manifest. These boundaries act as a container for abundance rather than a barrier against scarcity: they create the specific conditions required for deep rest and long-term growth. The focus shifts from the shadow of past injuries to forging a life that mirrors true potential. Boundaries serve as a vital framework for nurturing ambitions, providing the structure to pursue what truly matters and transforming fear-driven reactions into empowered, strategic actions. By prioritizing internal needs, an environment is cultivated where one can flourish rather than shrink.

Taking up space is an inherent right. In the state of mastery, there is no longer a need to apologize for presence or to voice desires tentatively. The role of the protagonist in one's own life story is fully embraced, moving out of the shadows of a supporting role to inhabit an identity defined by confidence. Sincerity replaces hesitation. When the voice is used with clarity, it adds tangible value and commands acknowledgment: defining what it means to engage with the world confidently and unapologetically.

True empowerment is not found in the eradication of fear, but in the capacity to move through it. Courage is fear in motion. The nervous system often triggers a protective response designed for a much more primitive environment than the modern societal structures we navigate today. In these moments, fear is recognized as a biological relic: a signal to be acknowledged rather than a reason to retreat.

The resulting clarity of structure delineates where one person ends and another begins, which is the foundational requirement for independence. With this distinction, trust in personal decision-making grows: both "yes" and "no" are embraced with equal conviction. Interactions are navigated with a sense of physiological security, knowing that well-being is protected. This trust clears the path for living freely within a self-crafted framework, promoting a harmonious balance between the self and others. By establishing these standards, the internal system feels secure enough to move forward with purpose, ensuring fear becomes a passenger rather than the driver.

From Wounds to Wholeness: Healing and Personal Reclamation

The pursuit of mastery is inseparable from the reclamation of the inner self. In this stage, freedom feels like a gentle refuge: a space where the inner child can finally feel safe, seen, and deeply valued. Boundaries form the walls of this sanctuary, granting you the security you may have lacked in the past but have the power to provide now. As you engage in the work of reparenting with unwavering love, patience, and perseverance, you are not merely healing old wounds. You are nurturing your essence and offering the care you once longed for. Every inner guideline serves as a gentle embrace, reassuring the inner child of their worthiness of protection and love. Engaging in therapeutic practices like journaling or mindfulness can further support this process, allowing for a deeper, more resilient connection with yourself.

Freedom from toxic dynamics involves breaking free from cycles of emotional, verbal, or financial abuse. In this context, boundaries become the foundation of self-respect, reconstructing what was eroded by detrimental environments. You rediscover safety within your own mind and body: a physical realization that loyalty does not necessitate self-sacrifice. This newfound security opens the path to the trust and love you deserve, free from manipulation. You reclaim your voice, articulating needs without fear of dismissal or retaliation. The "freedom" found here is the ability to speak your truth and have it feel like a release rather than a risk.

The shift from anxious or avoidant attachment styles toward secure ones fundamentally alters your connectivity to others. The spaces you honor serve as the blueprint for this transformation, helping to redefine your identity beyond past traumas or inherited roles. As you embrace this framework, a sense of inherent worth flourishes, bringing confidence and a true sense of belonging. The past no longer dictates your present: instead, it guides your path toward wholeness. Knowing what you value and protecting your space helps you understand yourself more deeply and nurture relationships built on genuine, autonomous ties. This is the ultimate freedom: the ability to belong to yourself while remaining deeply connected to the world.

From Surviving to Thriving: Celebrating the Journey

Thriving is the ultimate act of reclamation. It is the moment when a "no" that once felt like a risk becomes a milestone of integrity. The progression from surviving to thriving is a fundamental evolution: a transition from a life defined by defense to one defined by design. By choosing to protect your energy and values, you have rewritten your narrative. This healing manifests in the quiet, calm certainty with which you handle daily challenges. Your worth is no longer a commodity up for negotiation or a variable tied to external approval. This grounded confidence stands as the definitive testament to your resilience.

You now set the standard for living authentically. The requirement for external permission has dissolved, replaced by an internal authority that requires no justification. This is the sensory reality of freedom: the ability to navigate the world without the exhausting weight of others' expectations. Where you once drifted in the current of other people's needs, you now move with a steady, intentional direction. Your boundaries have transitioned from defensive walls into a clear, intentional shoreline that defines the territory of your life.

This transformation extends beyond the individual to influence the health of entire communities. When you stop absorbing the emotional static of a system, you force that system to recalibrate. By prioritizing your own needs, you cultivate an environment in which you flourish rather than shrink, creating a permission structure for others to do the same. Choosing self-respect over reactive compliance provides the essential framework for healthier, more honest connections built on genuine ties rather than obligation.

The final shift of freedom is the move from a life of reaction to a life of agency. It feels like the difference between being tossed by the tide and finally finding your footing on solid ground. You are no longer merely responding to the demands of the world. You are the architect of your own days, choosing what to build and what to leave behind. Freedom is the quiet, steady power of belonging to yourself completely. You have emerged from the noise of the collective current to inhabit a life that is, for the first time, entirely your own.

CHAPTER 15

AUTHENTIC, EMPOWERED LIVING

Authentic living is the natural outcome of honoring your boundaries over time. When your choices consistently reflect your values, life begins to feel less like something you are managing and more like something you are inhabiting fully. The pressure to perform or conform gradually fades, replaced by a steady confidence in who you are and what you stand for. In this chapter, we explore what it means to live from that place of clarity: where boundaries support your identity, your values shape your decisions, and your life reflects the person you have become.

Authenticity and Boundaries: Living True to Yourself

Authenticity emerges when your actions, choices, and interactions align with your core self instead of being shaped by societal pressure or external expectations. This way of living creates a genuine presence in each moment, unfiltered and grounded. It forms the foundation for a life of satisfaction and meaning. At its core, this requires staying intimately connected to personal beliefs. A framework built from deliberate choices sustains this integrity, empowering you to reject outside forces attempting to shape you into a version that does not resonate with your truth. By establishing these standards, you assert autonomy and protect your identity while carving out the space required for self-preservation.

Living with clear anchors to your values comes with immediate benefits. A deeper sense of fulfillment emerges as choices consistently parallel the real self, bringing lasting inner calm. This harmony between actions and values elevates relationships to a higher level of quality. Open communication and the acknowledgment of personal limits build trust and closeness. People are naturally drawn to the transparency that emanates from honesty, forging interactions that are both meaningful and reciprocal.

To uphold this truth consistently, it is crucial to establish personal habits that anchor you to your values. These rituals may include beginning each day with a moment of reflection or dedicating specific time to pursuits that ignite passion. Regular inner work is indispensable. Frequently reviewing whether actions mirror core principles allows for the adjustments needed to stay true to yourself. This ongoing calibration ensures life remains an embodiment of your deepest aspirations.

Aligning Actions with Authenticity

Reflect on your past week during a quiet moment of transition:

- Was there a moment that felt undeniably you?

- Was there a time you felt pulled away from your values by the "current" of others?

- What voices, such as internal doubts or external pressures, shaped those choices?

- How might refining your expectations help you stay closer to your true self next time?

To ground this reflection, consider the intentional shifts made by others who chose design over drift:

Everyday Stories: When Boundaries Become Real

Choosing Depth Over Urgency

Sarah worked as a graphic designer in a high-pressure firm where her role had devolved into a series of reactive, last-minute revisions. Because of poor planning in other departments, she was constantly forced to rush her work, compromising the professional standards she held for herself. Her authenticity was being drained by the friction between her commitment to quality and a culture of perpetual "emergencies." Her turning point was establishing a "Mastery Window": she designated the first four hours of her day as unreachable for non-critical requests. By guarding this time, she ensured that her primary energy was spent on the innovative work that met her internal standard of excellence. She shifted from being a reactive technician to a proactive creator, ensuring her daily labor reflected her actual talent rather than just her availability.

Choosing Values Over Belonging

Kenji lived in a social circle where consumerism and expensive nightlife were the primary languages of connection. For him, authenticity meant aligning his habits with his environmental convictions, even when it made him the "inconvenient" friend. By setting boundaries around how he spent his money and time, he moved from being a passenger in a culture of waste to being the architect of a sustainable life. Over time, this choice naturally realigned his social world. As he spent more time hiking, kayaking, and biking, he found a community of like-minded people who valued the same stillness and nature. His "no" to a consumerist weekend was the "yes" that allowed him to belong to a community where he no longer had to hide his values to fit in.

Record your thoughts in whatever way feels natural: writing, sketching, or voice-recorded notes. This is not a self-criticism exercise; it is an observation of where choices match the true self and where they drift, allowing for more intentional steps forward.

Empowerment Through Boundaries: Owning Your Life

Empowerment is the driving force that moves you toward a life defined by confidence. When viewed through the lens of boundaries, it means taking full command of your decisions and expressing your intent without reservation. By drawing a clear line, you state that your space, time, and emotional energy are deserving of respect. This establishes the framework for self-confidence, ensuring your voice is both heard and valued. Empowering yourself through these personal guidelines reshapes your interaction with the world, enabling you to follow your aspirations with courage.

To fully harness this empowerment, master the skill of assertive decision-making. Whether you are in a boardroom, a family gathering, or a social setting, articulate your needs clearly and calmly. Let your words carry quiet conviction, grounded in an unshakable sense of purpose. Instead of defaulting to silence, frame your communication through your own perspective. Using "I" statements shifts the focus inward, turning conversations into honest observations rather than confrontations. This internal alignment reinforces your ability to hold firm boundaries even in the face of opposition.

The ripple effect of empowerment extends to broader life transformations. As you strengthen your personal standards, you will find yourself engaging with new opportunities with more eagerness. Whether embracing a career shift or acquiring a new skill set, empowerment uncovers paths that were previously hidden. It amplifies leadership capabilities, enriching the ability to lead teams and families with empathy and decisiveness. As boundaries honor your limits, they also reveal your potential and encourage you to pursue roles that align with your values.

Everyday Stories: When Boundaries Become Real

Raising the Standard

Amara, a senior project lead, realized her life was being dictated by the "emergency" cultures of others. Her decision to cease responding to non-critical communications after 6:00 PM reestablished her baseline for professional respect. This boundary required her department to become more organized, as she refused to serve as the safety net for poor planning. This shift in her availability increased her professional value: her team learned to respect her time and arrive at meetings fully prepared.

Spending in Alignment

Alex began noticing how much of his social life revolved around spending money in ways that never truly felt right to him. Weekend plans often meant expensive restaurants, nightlife, and impulse purchases that clashed with his growing commitment to environmental responsibility. For a long time, he went along with it to maintain the sense of belonging within his circle.

Eventually, he made a quiet shift. Alex began setting clearer boundaries around how he spent both his time and his money. Instead of defaulting to the same social patterns, he started organizing activities that reflected his real interests: hiking local trails, kayaking on nearby lakes, and spending long afternoons outdoors. As his habits changed, so did the company he kept. Some friendships faded naturally, while new ones formed with people who valued the same slower pace and connection to nature. By honoring his convictions, Alex discovered that authenticity does not isolate you. It simply guides you toward the places where you no longer need to hide who you are.

Continuous Growth: Evolving Your Boundary Practices

A well-designed life functions like a flourishing garden: alive, evolving, and shaped by intentional care. Such a life requires a commitment to ongoing cultivation: pruning habits that no longer serve the current season and planting new commitments that match shifting needs. Through patience and consistent attention, this practice develops into a living reflection of your values. Growth in this context involves embracing new experiences and allowing feedback to drive transformation.

Gardens are defined by their seasonality, and your personal standards must reflect the same natural rhythms. There are periods of rapid expansion that require firm trellises for support, and there are seasons of necessary die-off where old commitments must be cleared to make room for new life. Pruning is not an act of loss; it is a strategic redirection of energy toward what is currently vital. In a season of reclamation, your boundaries may feel firm and protective, acting as the necessary fencing to guard a vulnerable harvest. As you mature, these structures may become more flexible, allowing for cross-pollination and new growth while remaining rooted in your core integrity.

To promote this evolution, set progressive objectives that challenge you to expand your comfort zone. These goals might start with the simple act of declining a minor request and build toward reconfiguring the more significant structures of your life. Regular self-assessments are the tools of this trade. They allow you to evaluate whether your current limits are still serving your growth or if they have become root-bound and restrictive. A weekly review provides the space to examine instances when your lines were tested and how your response aligned with your integrity.

Everyday Stories: When Boundaries Become Real

Choosing Honest Transitions

For years, Mateo was a staple of his local bowling league. It was a routine that served him well when he needed a consistent social outlet. However, as his interests shifted toward environmental work and quiet reflection, the Tuesday night commitment began to feel like a weight. Instead of just disappearing or making excuses, Mateo spoke to his teammates with honesty. He expressed how much he valued the years of laughter and the strength of their friendships, but he explained that he needed to clear space for new hobbies that were calling to him. He made it a point to ask about staying in touch outside the league, ensuring his friends knew that while he was stepping away from the game, he wasn't stepping away from them. This honest communication turned a potential ending into a respectful transition.

Designing New Traditions

As Fatima started her own family, she realized the tradition of holiday travel was no longer sustainable. It left her exhausted and with little time to enjoy her children. To honor the needs of her household, she reached out to her parents to share her decision: she would be establishing a permanent home base for the holidays. Fatima spoke with deep empathy, acknowledging that this shift was significant for her as well as her parents, while simultaneously remaining clear that her decision was not up for debate. She invited both her parents and in-laws over for a brunch the weekend following the holiday to create a dedicated space for connection that didn't compromise her energy. By leading with love instead of seeking consensus, she ensured a new legacy could grow without severing the old.

Maintaining this evolving alignment ensures you stay balanced even when the environment around you changes. Your boundaries are the supports that steady your path, opening the way to a more grounded and intentional existence. As you progress, allow your standards to change as you do. Honoring your present needs opens the door to self-discovery and ensures that your life remains entirely your own.

Creating a Life That Honors Your Values

Making choices that align with your deepest principles provides a unique sense of clarity. In these moments, your actions embody who you truly are, and each decision supports a life shaped by authenticity rather than expectation. This alignment is not accidental; it is a deliberate construction, crafted through an honest exploration of what truly matters. This process begins by defining your core principles: the deep-seated guides that steer your actions and resolutions.

To really anchor your belief system and live out these core values, many people find power in a personal values manifesto. This is not an academic exercise but a written declaration of the non-negotiables that govern your life. It acts as a permanent reference point, ensuring your daily decisions mirror your long-term vision. When you set goals driven by value rather than mere ambition, you plant the seeds for a life that is both sustainable and fulfilling. Incorporating routines that reinforce these principles, such as a morning period of centering or an evening reflection, ensures your path remains consistent with your integrity.

In every decision, your values serve as a functional compass. You can utilize these beliefs to navigate complex choices with confidence. For example, when evaluating a career opportunity, an objective analysis includes more than financial gain; it assesses how the role aligns with your requirements for integrity and personal growth. Value-driven decisions are practical and pervasive, from the products you consume to the relationships you choose to nurture.

Crafting a lifestyle that honors your values involves designing both your personal and professional existence around these tenets. This often requires adjusting your work-life balance to prioritize family or seeking projects that align with a dedication to community service. You might choose to reshape your home into a space that fosters calm and creativity, or select a career path that honors your ethical standards. These shifts gradually shape a life where daily choices reflect what truly matters to you.

A life built on deliberate intent resembles a woven tapestry where the outward expression perfectly mirrors the inward belief. Authenticity is the result of this consistency. As you traverse this path, remember that your values are not static. They evolve as you grow. Embracing this evolution allows your values to guide you toward a life of profound fulfillment and sincerity.

Navigating Diverse Environments with Integrity

Living genuinely across different settings requires a sophisticated balance: honoring the cultural norms of a space without abandoning the internal standards you have built. This is not about becoming a chameleon to avoid friction; it is about practicing principled adaptability. You can move through diverse social and professional environments with sincerity by remaining anchored to your core while respecting the traditions and customs of others.

This balance is maintained through observant presence. By practicing attentive listening and keen observation, you learn to understand the "language" of a room. This allows you to engage respectfully without sacrificing your truth. In social settings, you can bridge the gap between your inner self and the external environment by sharing anecdotes that reflect your values or by posing open-ended questions that invite meaningful dialogue. These strategies transform casual encounters into opportunities for genuine connection.

If external pressures to conform begin to pull you away from your values, those values serve as a steadying anchor. Staying true to yourself involves affirming your rights and establishing the clear boundaries that safeguard your individuality. As your confidence grows, you will find that the world does not just accept your steadfastness; it begins to respect it. You move through the world with a quiet center, acknowledging the richness of various environments while firmly maintaining the integrity of your own path.

Celebrating Your Journey to Freedom

True freedom is forged through the cumulative power of your choices. Each instance where you chose integrity over conformity serves as a milestone of your liberation. Whether it was a quiet decision to trust your own judgment or a public stand for your personal standards, every act was a reclamation of self. Recognizing these victories validates your progress and reinforces your new reality. Reflecting on the moments you prioritized your needs without guilt transforms those experiences into a source of enduring strength. They are the living evidence of your evolution.

I remember when this shift first took hold in my own life. It wasn't a grand, cinematic moment; it was a simple "no" to a request that would have drained my remaining energy. I felt the familiar pull of guilt and the urge to over-explain, but instead, I sat with the discomfort. In that silence, I realized that I wasn't being difficult; I was being honest. Since then, I have repeated this process hundreds of times. Where the first instance spiked my cortisol and sent adrenaline coursing through my system in anticipation of a conflict, I now experience no physiological change. Honesty has become my natural state. Seeing that same clarity take root in your life is the greatest success of this work and it is absolutely possible and accessible for you.

While acknowledging milestones provides momentum, your ability to navigate friction is what secures your freedom. Maintaining a commitment to a growth mindset by abandoning self-criticism and judgment paves the way for resilience and consistent progress. When you stop viewing a setback as a moral failing, it becomes a diagnostic tool. Each challenge provides the data necessary to refine your boundaries and sharpen your discernment. By objectively analyzing these moments without the weight of shame, you transform obstacles into the insights that fortify your internal standards.

Every victory deserves to be marked as a point of personal record. These moments are the building blocks of a self-governed life. Celebrating these wins is a deliberate act of reinforcement. It signals to your subconscious that you are no longer a person who compromises for comfort; instead, you are a person who lives by design. These acknowledgments solidify your commitment to a life that belongs entirely to you.

As this chapter draws to a close, remember that authenticity is a living practice. You refine and rediscover it every day. Each choice to honor your values and each pause to listen to your internal voice deepens the story of who you truly are. These insights now ripple through your daily rhythms, your relationships, and the quiet moments that reveal what matters most. The journey continues as you carry these lessons forward into a life that is not only genuine but fully yours.

Conclusion

The Architecture of Liberty

As you reach the end of this journey, reflect on the transformative reality you have constructed. The ability to *Say No* and *Set Boundaries* is more than a social skill: it is the ultimate expression of self-respect. You have built a foundation of guilt-free limits that do not isolate you, but instead support a life of peace and purpose. By honoring these principles, you ensure that your worth, time, and energy are no longer up for negotiation.

Throughout this process, you have reclaimed your voice. You have learned that clarity is a form of kindness and that protecting your internal space is the only way to engage deeply with the world. You have moved past the exhausted state of overwhelm into a life of reciprocal relationships. These connections now flourish because they are built on mutual respect rather than silent resentment. You have the tools to decide who and what deserves access to your life, and that choice is yours alone.

The path to empowerment is illuminated by the choices you make to protect your spirit. This transition was made possible by your willingness to navigate discomfort and your refusal to carry the weight of unearned guilt. This shift in your internal and external world is not a temporary phase: it is a fundamental evolution of your identity.

See yourself stepping into days shaped entirely by your own design. Face life's challenges with a steady confidence grounded in the certainty that your requirements for peace are non-negotiable. This vision is within your reach, but remember that sovereignty is a practice, not a destination. Be patient with yourself as you integrate these techniques into your daily rhythm. Mastery is built through small, consistent actions and the grace you show yourself during the learning process.

Maintain this momentum by treating your boundaries as living principles. Continue to evaluate what supports your well-being, adapting your standards as your circumstances evolve. Regular self-assessment keeps your expectations aligned with your growth. This process of reflection and adaptation is what sustains harmony over a lifetime.

I want to express my deepest gratitude for your decision to walk this path with me. I recognize that your worth, time, and energy are your most precious resources, and I am honored that you chose to spend them within these pages. Your dedication to exploring these boundaries and seeking a more empowered life is inspiring. While this portion of our journey ends here, the practice of sovereignty is a lifelong endeavor. You are part of a collective of individuals who refuse to compromise their truth for the sake of convenience.

There is a profound, unshakable power in living on your own terms. Your boundaries are the keys that have finally unlocked your Freedom. Carry this certainty with you: you are the primary authority in your life. You are free to occupy your space, protect your peace, and exist exactly as you choose. Here is to a future defined by your authenticity and the boundless power of a self-governed life.

Use Your Voice. Change A Life.

Whether you've read this guide straight through or returned to it in the moments you needed it most, you now have something powerful: words you can rely on when it matters.

Even one clear, grounded response can shift a conversation, protect your energy, and begin to change the way others relate to you.

Please Help Someone Else Find the Words They Need.

If this guide has helped you speak up, respond differently, or navigate a moment with more clarity, I would be truly grateful if you shared that experience in a brief Amazon review. Your review helps this guide reach others who are still searching for what to say and how to say it.

Simply scan the QR code below to leave a quick review or star rating.

What to share? Specific stories carry the most weight.

Did a script help you respond differently than you normally would?
Did you say less instead of over-explaining?
Did you hold your ground in a way that felt new or unfamiliar?

Even one small shift can be the exact example someone else needs to see what's possible.

Thank you for your trust and for doing the hard work of using your voice, one conversation at a time.

With deepest gratitude,

REFERENCES

"A Guide to Setting Better Boundaries." *Harvard Business Review*. n.d. https://hbr.org/2022/04/a-guide-to-setting-better-boundaries.

"6 Reasons Why Managers Need Negotiation Skills." *Harvard Business School Online*. n.d. https://online.hbs.edu/blog/post/negotiation-skills-for-managers.

"8 Ways to Stop Being a People-Pleaser." *Verywell Mind*. n.d. https://www.verywellmind.com/how-to-stop-being-a-people-pleaser-5184412.

"Assertive Behaviour That Brings Success in the Workplace." *The Hub Events*. n.d. https://www.thehubevents.com/resources/examples-assertive-behaviour.

"Assertive Communication." *Psychology Tools*. n.d. https://www.psychologytools.com/resource/assertive-communication.

"Be True to Yourself: Your Guide to Authenticity and Growth." *Resilient Stories*. n.d. https://resilientstories.com/be-true-to-yourself.

"Being Assertive: Reduce Stress, Communicate Better." *Mayo Clinic*. n.d. https://www.mayoclinic.org/healthy-lifestyle/stress-management/in-depth/assertive/art-20044644.

"Boundaries." *Psychology Today*. n.d. https://www.psychologytoday.com/us/basics/boundaries.

"Effects of Narcissistic Abuse." *Verywell Mind*. n.d. https://www.verywellmind.com/effects-of-narcissistic-abuse-5208164.

"Emotional Intelligence Is Rooted in Healthy Boundaries." *Heartmanity*. n.d. https://blog.heartmanity.com/emotional-intelligence-is-rooted-in-healthy-boundaries.

"Fear of Rejection: Signs, Effects, & How to Overcome." *Choosing Therapy*. n.d. https://www.choosingtherapy.com/fear-of-rejection.

"How to Find a Narcissistic Abuse Support Group." *Verywell Mind*. n.d. https://www.verywellmind.com/how-to-find-a-narcissistic-abuse-support-group-5271477.

"How to Set Boundaries and Why It Matters for Your Mental Health." *UC Davis Health*. n.d. https://health.ucdavis.edu/blog/cultivating-health/how-to-set-boundaries-and-why-it-matters-for-your-mental-health/2024/03

"How to Set Boundaries as an Introvert and Still Be Kind." *Introvert Dear*. n.d. https://introvertdear.com/news/introverts-the-life-changing-power-of-setting-healthy-boundaries.

"How to Set Healthy Boundaries vs. Barriers." *Finding Happily*. n.d. https://findinghappily.com/healthy-boundaries-vs-barriers.

"How to Use Emotional Intelligence for Self-Care Boundaries." *LinkedIn*. n.d. https://www.linkedin.com/advice/1/how-can-you-use-emotional-intelligence-set-8b2tf.

"14 Assertiveness Scripts and Interpersonal Rights." *Dialectical Behavior Therapy*. n.d. https://dialecticalbehaviortherapy.com/interpersonal-effectiveness/assertiveness-scripts-and-interpersonal-rights.

"Internal and External Boundaries: Why They Matter and How to Set Them." *LinkedIn*. n.d. https://www.linkedin.com/pulse/internal-external-boundaries-why-matter-how-set-them-morrison-pt-dpt.

"Life Is a Project." *Life Is a Project*. n.d. https://lifeisaproject.com/tag/busy-professionals.

"Map It Out: Setting Boundaries for Your Well-Being." *Mayo Clinic Health System*. n.d. https://www.mayoclinichealthsystem.org/hometown-health/speaking-of-health/setting-boundaries-for-well-being

"Resilience: Build Skills to Endure Hardship." *Mayo Clinic*. n.d. https://www.mayoclinic.org/tests-procedures/resilience-training/in-depth/resilience/art-20046311.

"Self-Help Strategies for Social Anxiety." *Anxiety Canada*. n.d. https://www.anxietycanada.com/sites/default/files/adult_hmsocial.pdf.

"Setting Healthy Boundaries as a Form of Self-Care." *MS Center*. n.d. https://mscenter.org/article/setting-healthy-boundaries-as-a-form-of-self-care.

"Strategies for Overcoming Social Anxiety and Building Confidence." *Alison Weiner MD*. n.d. https://www.alisonweinermd.com/blog-posts/stepping-beyond-fear-strategies-for-overcoming-social-anxiety-and-building-confidence.

"The Art of Emotional Control: Strategies for Managing Emotions During Challenging Discussions." *Innovative Human Capital*. n.d. https://www.innovativehumancapital.com/article/the-art-of-emotional-control-strategies-for-managing-emotions-during-challenging-discussions.

"The Psychology of People-Pleasing." *Medium*. n.d . https://medium.com/clear-yo-mind/the-psychology-of-people-pleasing-cf9ae3299a15.

Turonova, Silvia. "3 Reasons Why We Fear Setting Boundaries and How to Overcome It." *Silvia Turonova*. n.d . https://silviaturon.com/3-reasons-why-we-fear-setting-boundaries-and-how-to-overcome-it.

Turonova, Silvia. "Four Ways Mindfulness Can Help with Better Boundaries." *ClearHeart PDX*. n.d.

Turonova, Silvia. "Your Mind Is Not Your Enemy: 3 Ways How to Better Manage Your Thoughts." *Silvia Turonova*. n.d.

"Emotional Hijacking: What Happens in Your Brain During Conflict." *Think Better*. n.d. https://thinkbetter.com.au/emotional-hijacking-what-happens-in-your-brain-during-conflict.

"Things to Stop Doing to Improve Your Personal Life." *Aware Care Durango*. n.d. https://www.awarecaredurango.com/post/things-to-stop-doing-to-improve-your-personal-life.

"Workplace Warriors: The Rise of Boundary-Setters in a Burnout Economy." *Forbes*. n.d. https://www.forbes.com/sites/dianehamilton/2025/01/07/workplace-warriors-the-rise-of-boundary-setters-in-a-burnout-economy.